JEAN-MICHEL BASQUIAT
THE NOTEBOOKS

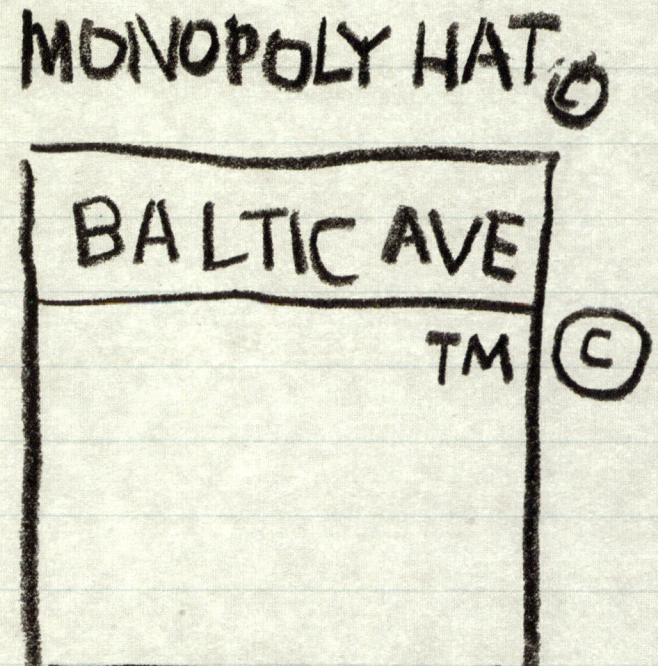

MONOPOLY HAT ©

BALTIC AVE

™ ©

Requests for permission to reproduce material from this work should be sent to
    Permissions, Princeton University Press

Published by Princeton University Press,
    41 William Street
    Princeton, New Jersey 08540
In the United Kingdom: 99 Banbury Road, Oxford OX2 6JX

press.princeton.edu

In association with No More Rulers
nomorerulers.com   @nomorerulers

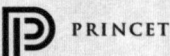 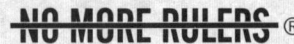

The NO MORE RULERS mark and logo are registered trademarks of
No More Rulers, Inc. All Rights Reserved

Cloth ISBN 978-0-691-16789-3

Library of Congress Control Number: 2014959951

British Library Cataloging-in-Publication Data is available

This book has been composed in DIN Pro

Printed on acid-free paper.

Printed in Malaysia

10 9 8 7 6

JEAN-MICHEL BASQUIAT
THE NOTEBOOKS

EDITED BY LARRY WARSH

PRINCETON UNIVERSITY PRESS

Princeton & Oxford

~~NO MORE RULERS~~ ®

INTRODUCTION

In the Beginning

You could think of this book as energy—a concentrated dose of pure, creative energy contained between unassuming black-and-white-marbled covers. Jean-Michel Basquiat's notebooks are not sketchbooks, and they weren't intended for doodling. They're a summary of his most carefully articulated, intimate, and poetic thoughts. With words and images rendered in ink, markers, paint, and oil sticks, the notebooks are where Jean-Michel clarified his voice in a highly visual way. For him, the books were a separate practice, distinct from the work he did on the street or in the studio. Their value was in the creative process they facilitated, as well as in their status as objects or works of art in their own right. They captured the essence of his mind, what he was thinking in the moment. As art critic Rene Ricard wrote in an unpublished essay:

> In these notebooks one can chart the process of refinement as Basquiat purges himself of syntax and the received structure of language, almost the entire apparatus of style, to arrive at the final and irreducible few blocks of substance that comprise his mature work.

How these notebooks came into my hands (and yours) is a story in itself.

In the early 1980s, I was living on Astor Place in Lower Manhattan. I was introduced to Patti Astor and her legendary Fun Gallery, which became my entry point into the new world taking shape at the time. Patti was one of the core people on the downtown scene; she was spirited, smart, and passionate. The scene was bursting with frenetic energy. It was obvious that something historic was going on.

Rene Ricard was a major influence on me. He would drop by at all hours to discuss drawings or canvases, as late as 3 or 4 a.m. if a piece excited him. He would talk about its history, and in his own way communicate its energy. I was beginning to collect art, and in those days I had a voracious appetite for work by Keith Haring and Jean-Michel Basquiat. I felt comfortable with their work, which struck me as important. Living downtown, it felt right, and right at home.

I acquired the notebooks in the late 1980s, when things were really alive in the New York art world. I remember how aware I was of the future in that moment, and cognizant of the role that the notebooks would play in understanding Jean-Michel's work. His brilliance, his essence, was on those pages. The notebooks reflect his sophisticated sense of design, but also the importance of the word. Half-words, blocked and crossed-out words, and revised phrases all contribute to the play between the conscious and unconscious mind of the artist.

At that time it was hard for many people to grasp the art of that moment, and my choices as a collector were frequently questioned. The art of a particular period sometimes takes a decade or more to be understood. Culture always has to catch up.

And here we are, in the future.

The notebooks reveal Jean-Michel's preparations for his attack on the art world that was to follow. They are like Napoleonic battle plans. A phrase like "FAMOUS NEGRO ATHLETES ©," which would appear throughout his art, is shown to have originated here. The words on these pages found their way into Jean-Michel's larger works on paper as well as his canvases, and they reveal the crucial first step on his creative path as he moved from drawing to painting. In some instances Jean-Michel applied notebook pages, or photocopies of them, directly onto his canvases.

In a 1993 essay, Henry Geldzahler wrote:

> Jean-Michel lived a short life, but he left us with a lot of memorable work, an astonishing amount given the number of his working years. The ancient Greeks believed that lives were not tragically short or satisfyingly long; rather, they thought, each life is lived to its own termination, and should be valued in its own terms. One might think of him as a warrior who fell too soon in a battle not of his making.[1]

This facsimile edition includes eight of Jean-Michel's notebooks, plus a few loose notebook pages that came with them. Each page captures the flow of ideas and images in the artist's own hand. It is my hope that the notebooks will provide a foundation for viewing and understanding the work of Jean-Michel Basquiat, and will reveal important facets of his complex creative persona. While we can never have a complete picture of the inner workings of any artist, the words on these pages offer a glimpse of the soul that was Jean-Michel.

Larry Warsh

---

1. Henry Geldzahler, "Introduction," *Jean-Michel Basquiat: The Notebooks* (New York: Art + Knowledge, 1993), 8–10.

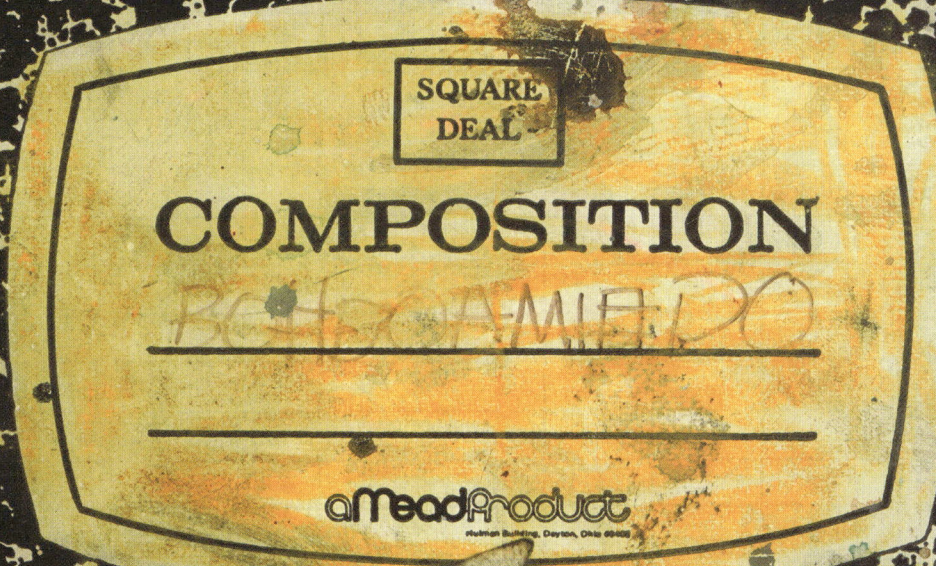

SQUARE
DEAL

COMPITION

aMeadProduct

CLASS PROGRAM

NAME _472-2073_ ADDRESS _5:00 7:30_

SCHOOL _265·E 4M·_ CLASS _2nd._

	TIME	FROM TO...	PERIOD 1	PERIOD 2	PERIOD 3	PERIOD 4	PERIOD 5	PERIOD 6	PERIOD 7	PERIOD 8
MONDAY	SUBJECT									
	ROOM									
	INSTRUCTOR									
TUESDAY	SUBJECT				255 1064					
	ROOM									
	INSTRUCTOR				CLAIRE					
WEDNESDAY	SUBJECT									
	ROOM									
	INSTRUCTOR									
THURSDAY	SUBJECT									
	ROOM									
	INSTRUCTOR									
FRIDAY	SUBJECT									
	ROOM									
	INSTRUCTOR									
SATURDAY	SUBJECT									
	ROOM									
	INSTRUCTOR									

No. 09-4160 • WIDE RULED with MARGIN

60 SHEETS • SIZE 9¾ IN. x 7½ IN.

AN ADVERTISEMENT FOR SODA

~~PENGUINS ARE LIKELY TO STAY WITH THE SAME MATE FOR MONTHS~~

~~FIRE WILL ATTRACT MORE ATTENTION THAN ANY OTHER CRY FOR HELP.~~

~~THIER DOGS THIER HARPOONS THIER WIVES~~

~~THE~~ THE AVERAGE MAN LAUGHS 15 TIMES A DAY.

THE GIANT GORILLA LYING ON THE PAVEMENT

THE DREAM WILL NEVER DIE ACCEPT THE REALITY OF LIVING IN THE STATE

~~RUSHED INTO THE LIMO BY SECRET SEVICE~~

IN A FRONTAL ATTACK

MILLING IN THE CROWD

TODAY HE ADMITTED TO BEING FOOLISH

RAN INTO THE TRAIN BEAT OUT THE FLAMES

~~THEY HAD TO~~

THEY FALLEN ASLEEP AND WERE INHALING THE SMOKE.

SLIGHT CRACK IN THE GAS LINE

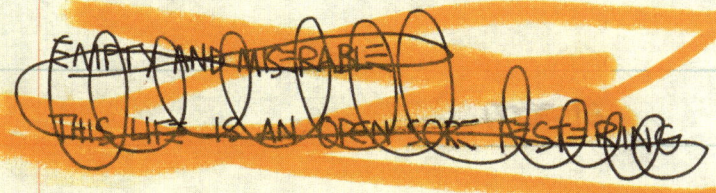
~~EMPTY AND MISERABLE~~
~~THIS LIFE IS AN OPEN SORE FESTERING~~

~~BRICK RUINS~~

~~TOMB HOLLOW MORTURARIES~~

~~VOICES OF AUTHORITY MAKE MAJOR CLAIMS~~

~~OTHERS FROM THE EAST~~

~~GATHER AROUND THEM~~

SHO

A BUS TICKET TO SCRANTON PENS.

~~BUR~~
~~CUR~~

~~IT DID AFFECT 8000 ACRES~~ ~~WEEK~~

REBUILDING THE ROAD NETWORK

LARGER AMOUNTS OF WOOD

WOOD FIBER FOR PAPER

WOOD EATING INSECTS

PAPER PRODUCTS

~~SURVIVAL RATE IS RUNNING 20 PERCENT~~

SHOELACES

MATCHES

THERE IS A RACE ON

~~NATIONAL DISARRAY~~

~~BARK THRU THE SERVICE OF ANOTHER~~

STAGECOACH /

~~SOMEHOW~~ RECOVER, ADAPT, SHIFT MONITOR

~~HIGHLY CONTROLLED CIRCUMSTANCES~~

~~THE BARONS IGNORED BY IT'S PREDECESSORS~~

~~NAY GOOD IN PROOF~~

~~MOST INVESTORS~~

AN ACTOR GETTING SHOT BY A MACHINE GUN
ADD TAPE WITH PLASTIC BAG ATTACHED TO CLOTH WITH PLATE ON SKIN

~~THIS KIND OF GREASE~~

~~TOOTH BRUSH~~

~~HOT FUDGE AND PEANUTS~~

THREE MISSING LINKS

THE BAR WAS REALLY RED WITH CHINESE PAPER CUTOUTS
AND WOOD PANELING
  THERE WAS A GLASS ARGUMENT AT THE POOL TABLE
IN THE BACK

"
  THAT'LL BE EIGHTY CENTS POP "

6 OR 7 OLD PUGS IN FELT

SHE LOOKED LIKE A VILLAN FROM TERRY AND THE PIRATES

FAMOUS NEGRO ATHELETES

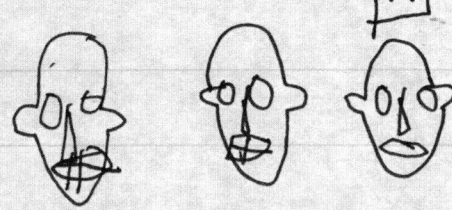

COMPOSITE DRAWINGS

JEAN   2   9

ARTO   2   9

TONY   2

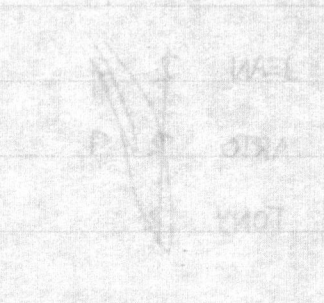

NEW ORLEANS ⎯⎯

BUS - 159.60 ⎯⎯⎯⎯

FRENCH QUARTER

THE COLUMNS — HOTEL

GANGSTER EMBLEMS

BLUE SUIT MARGARINE MEN

PUZZLE PIECE————

SUZANE EXPLAINED THE FILM TO ME

I'LL GIVE 20 LBS. OF OXYGEN FOR THAT DRAWING
YOU CAN'T SELL A HUMAN
YOU'VE DONE THIS SCRATCHING
THIS WAS NOT BLANK.

SCRATCHING ON THESE THINGS

I FEEL LIKE A CITIZEN IT'S TIME TO GO AND COME BACK A DRIFTER

~~IN THIS~~

I FEEL LIKE A CITIZEN IN THIS PARKING LOT COUNTY FAIR
IT'S TIME TO GREYHOUND AND COME BACK A DRIFTER
PUT IT ALL IN ONE BAG

I KNOW ONE DAY I'LL TURN THE CORNER AND I WON'T BE
READY FOR IT—

~~I CUR~~   I WAS CURSED FROM BIRTH.

POPULAR ~~CHEERLEADERS~~

I PLAYED THIER PART

AN ORPHAN   IF YOU KNEW MY COUNTERPARTS

A BIT TOO BITTER

NAIVE TO THE POINT OR 10 OR 11

~~BE~~ PHYSICAL COMPITITION

2 GIRLS JUST OUT OF ORANGEVILLE

BIG FARM/ COUNTRY HOUSE

I JUST WANT TO TALK ABOUT THESE GIRLS

PENALIZE

GET UP AND TALK OURSELVES ON A BIG STAGE

NEW CLOTHES ON ALL THE TIME

THEY ARENT DOING ANYTHING WRONG

TO A DIFFERANT DEGREE

HAS BEEN SUCH A LEADER

HAVE SCHOOL DANCE AND INVITE OTHER SCHOOLS

HAS'NT GOTTEN OVER IT

EVER TRUST

HAD IT ROUGH

UNDER THE LEAN·TO HIDING FROM SENTENIALS

BLUNTLY RESPONDS

CHARMED INTO BACKING THE SHOW

YOU'RE NEVER GOING TO BELIEVE THIS

GOLD HELMET

3·CARD SPREAD

ANTI· WHAT IT'S GOING TO BE LIKE

AT STAKES

CHIEF OF POLICE
STRIVING

LUMBERING WINO ON ASPHALT

FACE DOWN

LEAPSICKNESS

THE LAW OF LIQUIDS

THAT THORN IN MY HEAD NAGGING MY FISTS CLOSED

VICTIMS OF EMBELLISHED HISTORY

THE SPORES FLOATE

~~THE SPORES FLOATED ON EVERTHIN~~

~~THE SPORES FLOATED ON A POTATO FOAM~~

~~THET~~

SPORES FLOATED ON THE POTATO FOAMING THRU THE SKIN
~~THEY PUD ON SPOONS~~

THE GERMS ON A SPOON BEHIND THE OVEN

THE COLONY OF ROACHES IN THE OVEN LAY EGGS
UNDER TINFOIL IN THE OIL SWAMPS OF
BROILED STEAKS.
COOKED AND RECOOKED

RUBBER, MONEY AT A BUFFET
CARTS OF SHREDDED WHEAT

LOOT
BOOTY
RANSOM
 INFESTED BATHROOMS

HIGHER MONKEYS

SPRING ONIONS

THE HISTORY OF THE WORLD

AN EPILEPTIC SECRETARY ON TELEVISION

THAT MOBSTER STEVE'S GIRL

SCAN

DON'T SCREAM I WANT YOUR PURSE

IF YOU SCREAM WITHIN 60 SECONDS I'LL BE BACK

IN A DRAWER SCAN WE CAME UP WITH COPPER

IF A TRAMP STEALS A PURSE, IN THE FINANCIAL
DISTRICT
(

SCARECROW -

KAYO

IN THE TRIBAL PLAYGROUNDS SEVEN
TEST TUBES FELL INTO THE WRONG HANDS.

THIS MOMENTARY GAZELLE FREE-FRAMER

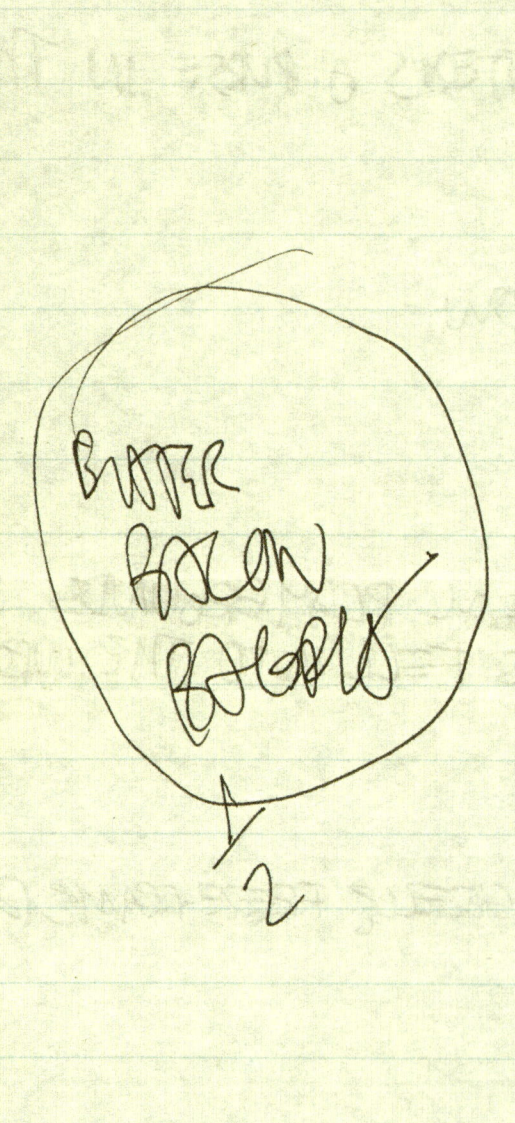

BUTTER
BACON
BAGELS

$\frac{1}{2}$

IF A DRUNK STEALS A PURSE IN THE FINANCIAL DISTRICT

~~KAYO'D BY A VALIANT SCARECROW~~

A RUBBER LION

~~SEWER COLONIES OF B~~

COARSE VOICES THRU 2-INCH SPEAKERS

MONOGRAMED UTENSILS

COLONIES OF BLACK RODENTS

FAKE SANDPAPER

SLEDGEHAMMER EYES

ROAD DINER

PLAY THE PART FOR HIS OWN REASONS

"WE PUT UP THE FAKE CACTUS EVERY YEAR AT THIS TIME

~~FIFTEEN MINUTES BEFORE THE BUS COMES~~"

A WHITESUIT COMES OUT OF THE KITCHEN WITH A LARGE
BAG OF OATS.
"THE BUS WILL BE HERE IN FIFTEEN MINUTES, MAKE SOME HOME
FRIES"

MAN ON A MOTORCYCLE TAKES A HAMBURG

THE MOTORCYCLE PULLS UP TO THE ROAD DINER MAN GETS OFF

ORDERS A HAMBURGER AND EGG HERO.

"WE PUT UP THE FAKE CACTUS EVERY YEAR AT THIS TIME"

A PROUD WORKER COMES OUT OF THE KITCHEN WITH A

LARGE BAG OF OATS

"

THE BUS WILL BE HERE IN 20 MINS./MAKE SOME HOME FRIES.

THE KITCHEN BOYS WHOOP AND YELL AND MAKE TWICE AS

MANY DONUTS.

THE MANAGER BRINGS SOME COLOR POSTCARDS OF ROCKS

FROM UNDERNEATH THE COUNTER BY THE MINTS AND CIGARS.

THE DISHWASHER PLUGS IN THE JUKEBOX AND FRIES HIS WET

HAND WITH A SHOCK.

THE LAW SITS DOWN FOR FREE SLICE OF PIE.

A MARBLE IN A SHOTGLASS

AFTER BREAKFAST HE STEALS A WALLET FROM DAY OLD DRUNK ON
SATURDAY MORNING ——

KERNELS OF CORN AS A FINAL OFFER ~~FOR DEFECTIVE RIFLES~~

THE EDITORS ARRESTED / MAGAZINE SHUT DOWN

THE WHOLE LITTLE TOWN WENT BED

IT ALL DEPENDS WHO YOU ARE ON WHAT STREET.

PODIUM SCALING HIS WAY TO A BED

HE HAD LEARNED TO IGNORE THE CRISP PART OF A 20 DOLLAR
BILL WITH AGE AND PLAYED NUMBERS FOR A FLIGHT TICKET.
REALLY OLD SHOES TAKE TRAINS.
THERE'S A FORTUNE IN NEWLYWEDS CROSSING THE
BORDER / MOST OF THEM WOULD TAPE THE MINERALS
TO THIER STOMACHS FOR HALF OF WHAT WAS
OFFERED. ~~THEY SECOND~~

HIS DAY LASTED TAFFY HOURS OF SLOW SMELLS STEAMING.

NO ONE PLAYED CHESS ANYMORE IT SEEMED MORE
/ VAPID TO RENT A CAR OR TO EAT AT
ROADSIDE WAR RESTAURANTS THAT SERVE
SURVIVAL DISHES.

LA STRADA

7:30

Bleeker

6:15
9:20

clemente

Diego

431685

MON # HALF HOUR →

223 —

#92394

19#

CRESENT →

MON 27TH —

#20 8TH MAY 8:15 AM →

HOLED UP IN RENTED BED WAITING ON NEW WORD

STATIC IS HARD ON VOICES BUT BLOCKS OUT CHAOS ON THE ~~BROADWAY~~ RUNWAY

LESS TO LOOK BACK ON LESS ~~ON CREDIT~~ HOT WATER ON CREDIT

I WAS LUCKY TO HAVE MY ~~M~~ CANVAS SUIT DRYCLEANED BEFORE THE RIOTS

~~WE THROW T~~

WE THREW PAMPHLETS AND BANNERS ON CARS OFF THE ROOF

~~WHOOPING ABOUT LOVERS AND THE PAST OVER EMOTIONAL COALS~~

IN CROSS SECTION OF ~~CRO~~ BAD ASTHETIC THE BLANK WINS OUT

HAMBURGER VETERANS IN MEDICAL CASEBOOKS

THESE BROWN PAPER JOHNNIES WITH RECORDED MEETINGS

~~WITH~~ MEMOS AND LETTERS

~~AN ADVERTISEMENT FOR SODA.~~

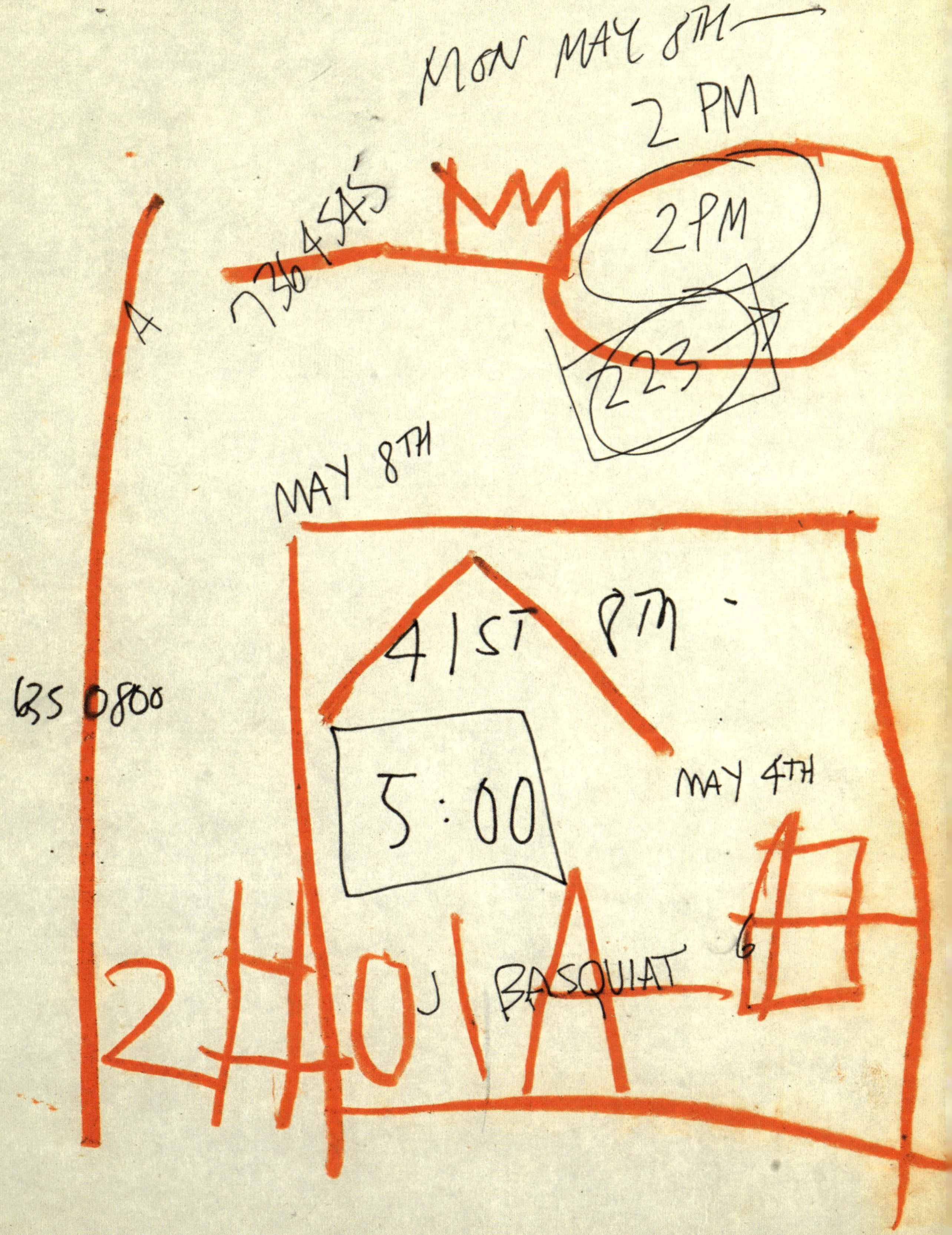
MON MAY 8TH
2 PM
2PM
223
A
736 4545
MAY 8TH
41ST
635 0800
5:00
MAY 4TH
J BASQUIAT

A TEXT ON TRANSLATING

PULL IN A DOG TO DRAW SANDPAPER/CENSOR HIS HABITS

~~XXXXX XXXXXXX~~

REALLY OLD SHOES TAKE TRAINS WITH THE MINERALS
TAPED TO THIER STOMACHS —

TIGHT / I'M A

SPRING

BOUNCING

HE PUTS A CHALK MARK ON HIS BACK AND WATCHES
HIM GET HIT BY A CAR FROM A SAFE DISTANCE.

KAYO IN THE LUNA PARK
FREEZE FRAME ON A DRUNK IN THE PIAZZA
THAT'S WHAT WE HAVE FOR PIGEONS
LUMBERING ON ASPHALT FACEDOWN
LEAPSICKNESSTHE LAW OF LIQUIDS.

FURTHER RESISTANCE TO THE FORCES OF THE
NATION OF LAW AND JUSTICE LIKE SOME
BAD STUPID COWBOY TURNING TO SEE THE
CLOCK ~~HHHH~~
   THE MAN IN THE WHITE HAT DROP IT
BEFORE DAWN WITH THEIR EXPRESSIONS
UNCHANGING SURROUNDED BY GUNS
THAT MELT SUNGLASSES

ECONOMICLY CRUMBLING ~~AN~~ FROM THE
B.29 RAY STALLING BEFORE IT ENDED
SUCESS HAD BEEN ACHIEVED.

A YELLOW FLASH A2STORY HOUSE
BLOWN TO PIECES / WE TOOK PICTURES
RAPIDLY / IT'S TIME TO GET OUT OF
HERE .

WHAT ABOUT THIS MODERN EDUCATION
FLASH CARDS AND ALL THAT.

ALBERT DENTON OWNED 51 PERCENT
OF FAMOUS WRESTLER

ISADORE HO

ONE CIVILLIAN HAD IT'S THROAT CU

A YOUTH WITH "CROW" SYNDROME:
~~AN AIR~~ (AN ATTRACTION TO SHINY OBJECTS/
SEES THE STONE AROUND HER NECK
                    FAT MONKEY

WALK FOR A QUARTER MILE/ LEFT 3 BLOCKS
TO A RED PICKET FENCE
GIVE THE BALD HEADED MAN A QUARTER
LOCK THE DOOR
SEE THIS REVERSE SPELLS THE OTHER WAY
THAT'S WHERE THE PEOPLE ARE
I THOUGHT YOU SAID WEDNESDAY

THIS BUM NAMED BALTIMORE
THIS VAGRANT NAMED CHICAGO
  A

A LOT OF BOWERY BUMS USED TO BE
EXECUTIVES—

SHE LOOKED HER THIRD EYE ACROSS THE
PARTY
       AT A SINSAE DIPLOT FROZE UNDER
PALM AT A BEACH RESORT 1000 MILES
AWAY—

HER VOICE TURNS INTO A BEGGAR IN SPAIN
A CRUCIFIX TRANSMITTING MONKEY HEAD
HYSTERIA INTO 20,000 TELEVISIONS—

AS THIEVES CUT THRU TWO THIN WALLS
TORCHING A HOLE THRU THE THIN METAL
OUTER COVERING .

THE TESTTUBE FALLS INTO GREEDY FINGERS
YELLOW FLASH
2 STORY HOUSE BLOWN TO PIECES
WE TOOK PICTURES
IT'S TIME TO . .
WALK DOWN 3/4 LEFT 3 BLOCK TO
A RED PICKET FENCE ,,,

GIVE THE BALDHEADED MAN A QUARTER
PULL IN A DOG TO DRAW SANDPAPER
CENSOR HIS HABITS
FREEZE-FRAME ON A ~~B~~ DRUNK IN THE
PLAZA
LEAPSICKNESS
THE LAW OF LIQUIDS .

RACKET IN HUMANS—

YOUTH HAS DICK CUT-OFF BY FOUR TRANSVESTITES
HE HAD BEEN RIDING WITH THEM ON
THE SUBWAYS AND FOUND HIMSELF
IN THE APT. THEY WERE SQUATTING
IN AND FELL ASLEEP.
SOMESO SOMEONE SCREAMS TURN DOWN THE
RADIO.

ANTS ON A CHICKEN BONE
WORKING MEN BREATHE THE DIRT OFF
THE BIG WHITE
WHITEBREAD WITH THE CENTER ATE OUT
A BALDHEADED BOY ON A BYCICLE.

TEXTILE WASTE
A BIG ALBINO BOY COMES INTO THE DINER
0 2 COKES FOR A BIG BODY.

DAYTIME WORLD RELIES ON NUMBERS—
MAKE IT MORE LIKELY FOR YOU TO SEE
PEOPLE FROM THE PAST.

THE JIG IS UP
SO SAY GOODBYE TO THE NIGHTMARE
ON AUTOMATIC PICOT

~~SINGED~~ SIGNED HIGHER SOURCES.

I AM NOT THE FAMOUS DISK
JOCKEY YOU WERE LEAD TO BELIEVE
I WAS —

~~MINIMUM 1000 BORDER ONE WE~~

MINIMUM 1000 BORDERS ONE WEEK NO EXCEPTIONS
SHE KNOWS ABOUT THE LAST TIME.

♫ ♫ ♪

AND NOW YOUR WINNER NO. 22 · CAL LANE

♫

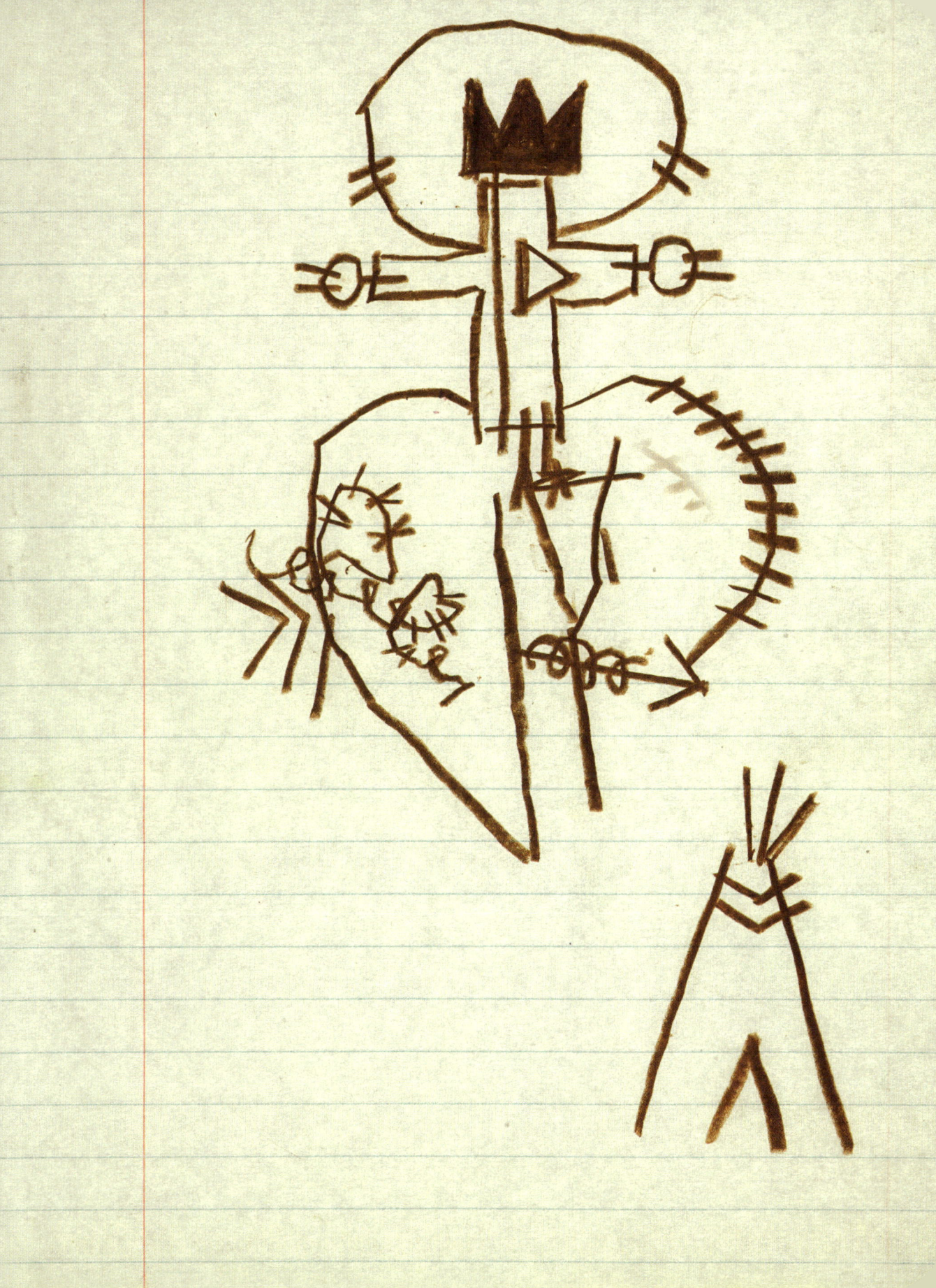

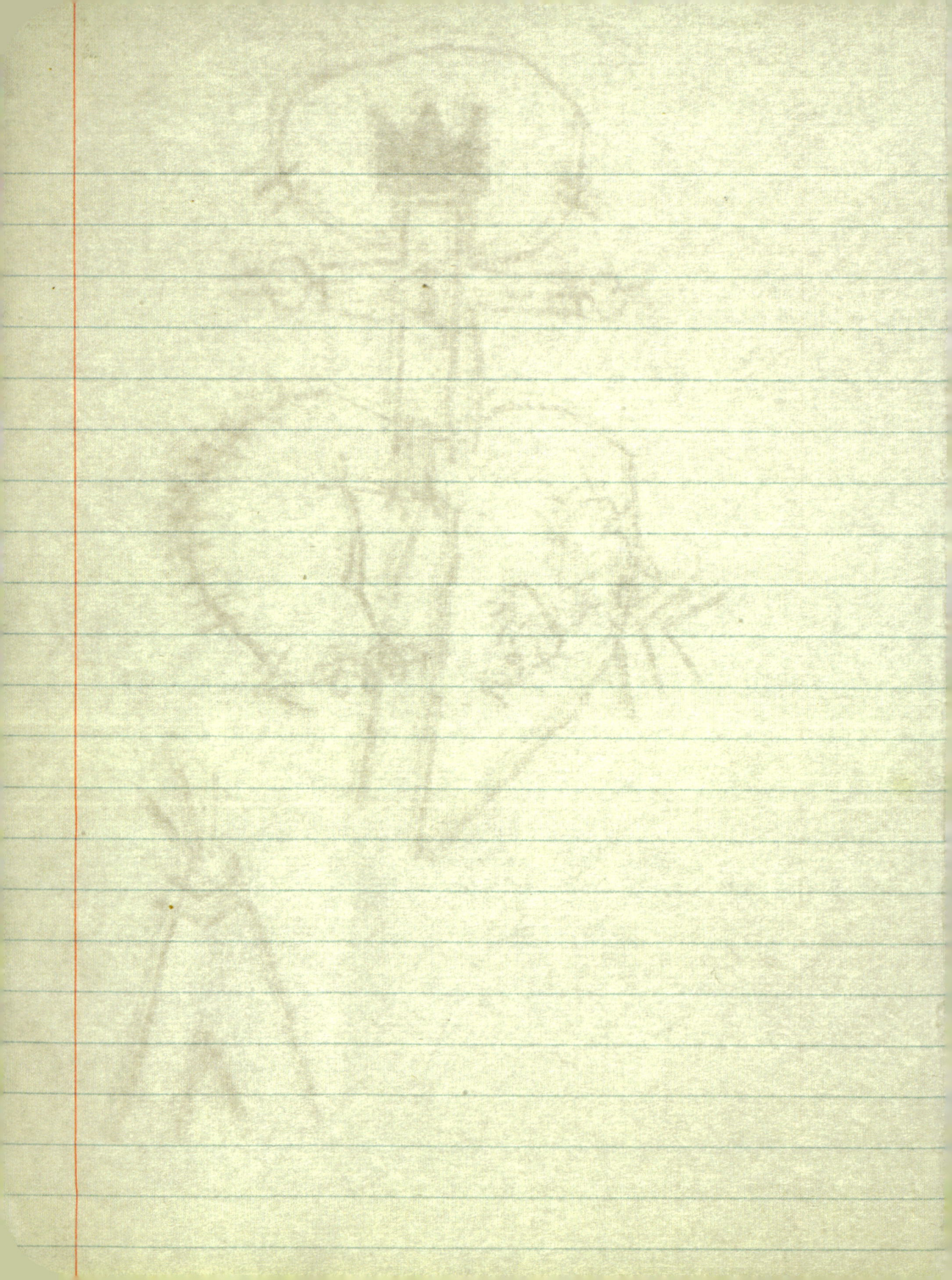

ONE UNIT OF FLATFOOT ON A FOOT BEAT

~~13Q~~

3 QUARTERS OF LEAD

THERE'S A ~~Y~~ SONG ON THE RADIO
WHERE THEY SAY WAVY HAIR INSTEAD OF BLACK

CONSIDERABLE CLOUDINESS

~~SO~~ IT WAS SUNG BY SOME WHITEGIRLS
20 YEARS LATER.

A STEP DOWN SOON. NO JOKE

■ VISE OF LOVE
A PILLAR OF SALT
~~IS THE~~ .
~~PANIC OF MALFUNFIC~~ .
PANIC OF MALFUNCTION .

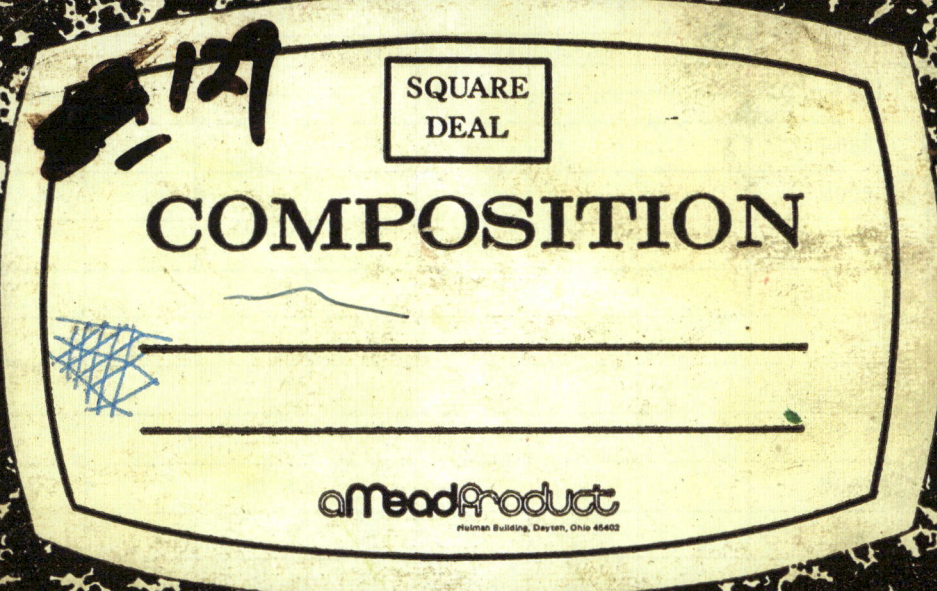

SQUARE
DEAL

COMPLACE

COMPOSITION

a Mead Product
Mead Building, Dayton, Ohio 45402

CLASS PROGRAM

NAME_____ ADDRESS_____

SCHOOL_____ CLASS_____

TIME	FROM TO...	PERIOD 1	PERIOD 2	PERIOD 3	PERIOD 4	PERIOD 5	PERIOD 6	PERIOD 7	PERIOD 8
MONDAY	SUBJECT								
	ROOM								
	INSTRUCTOR								
TUESDAY	SUBJECT								
	ROOM								
	INSTRUCTOR								
WEDNESDAY	SUBJECT								
	ROOM								
	INSTRUCTOR								
THURSDAY	SUBJECT								
	ROOM								
	INSTRUCTOR								
FRIDAY	SUBJECT								
	ROOM								
	INSTRUCTOR								
SATURDAY	SUBJECT								
	ROOM								
	INSTRUCTOR								

No. 09-4160 • WIDE RULED with MARGIN

60 SHEETS • SIZE 9¾ IN. x 7½ IN.

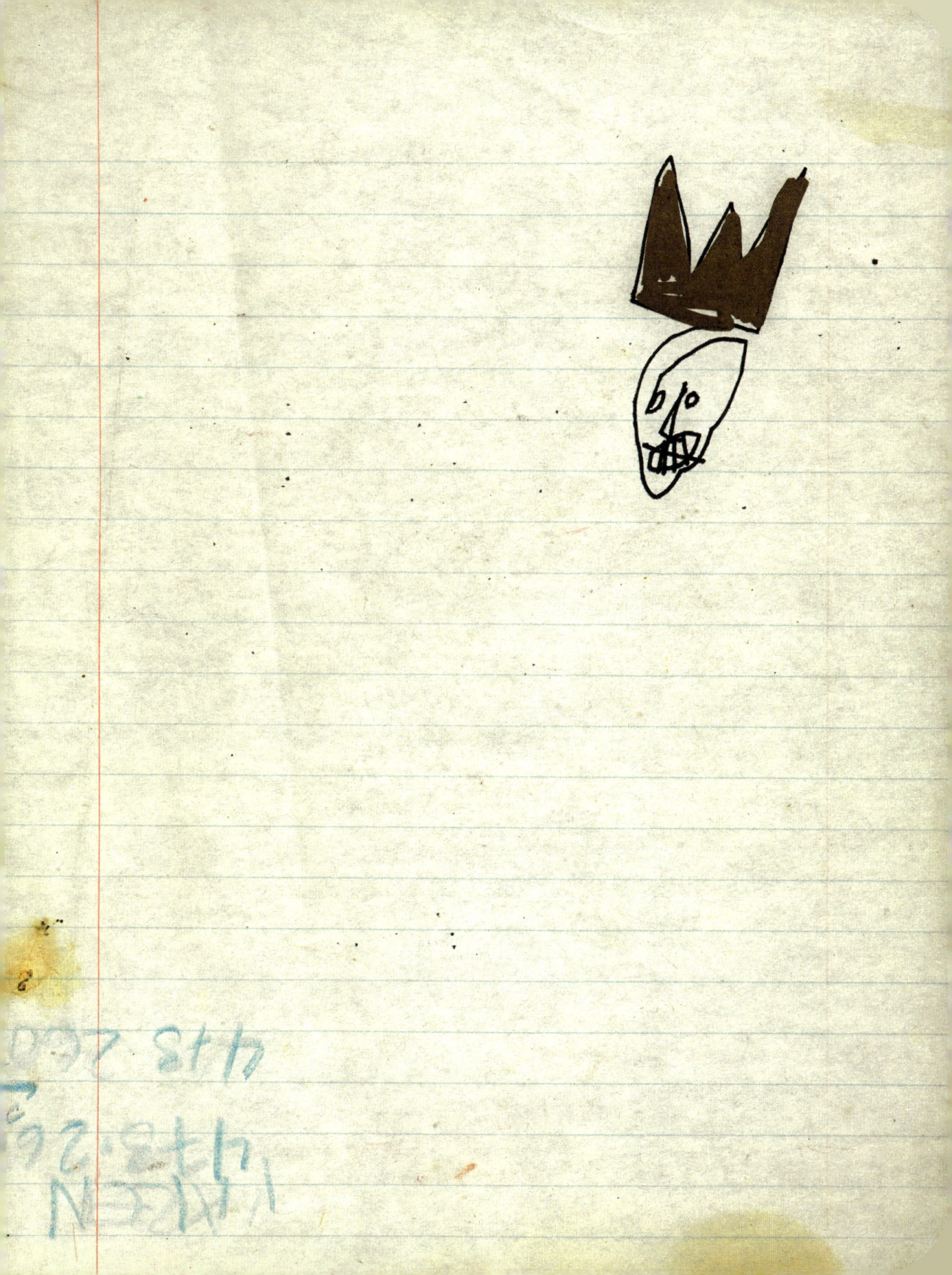

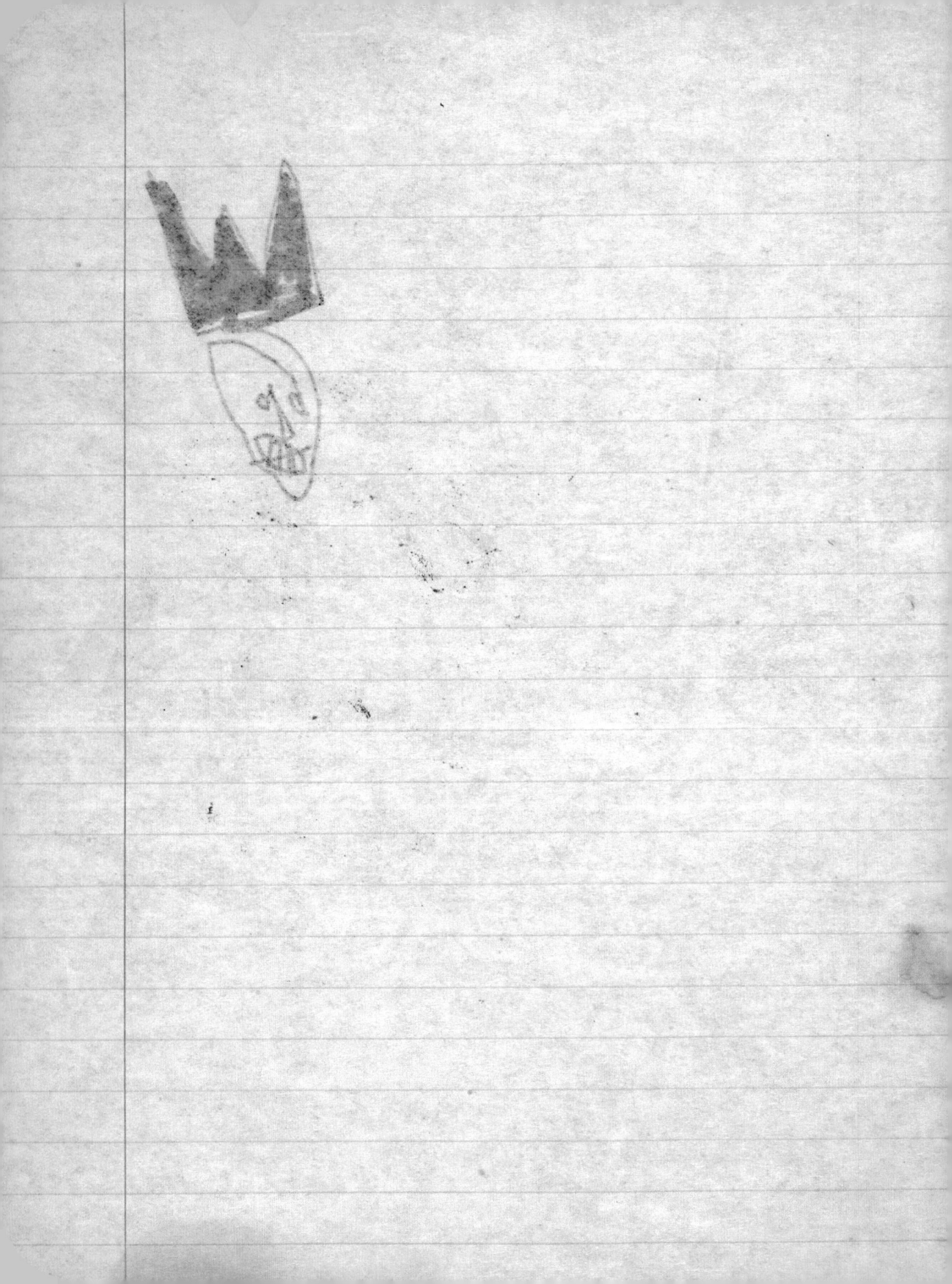

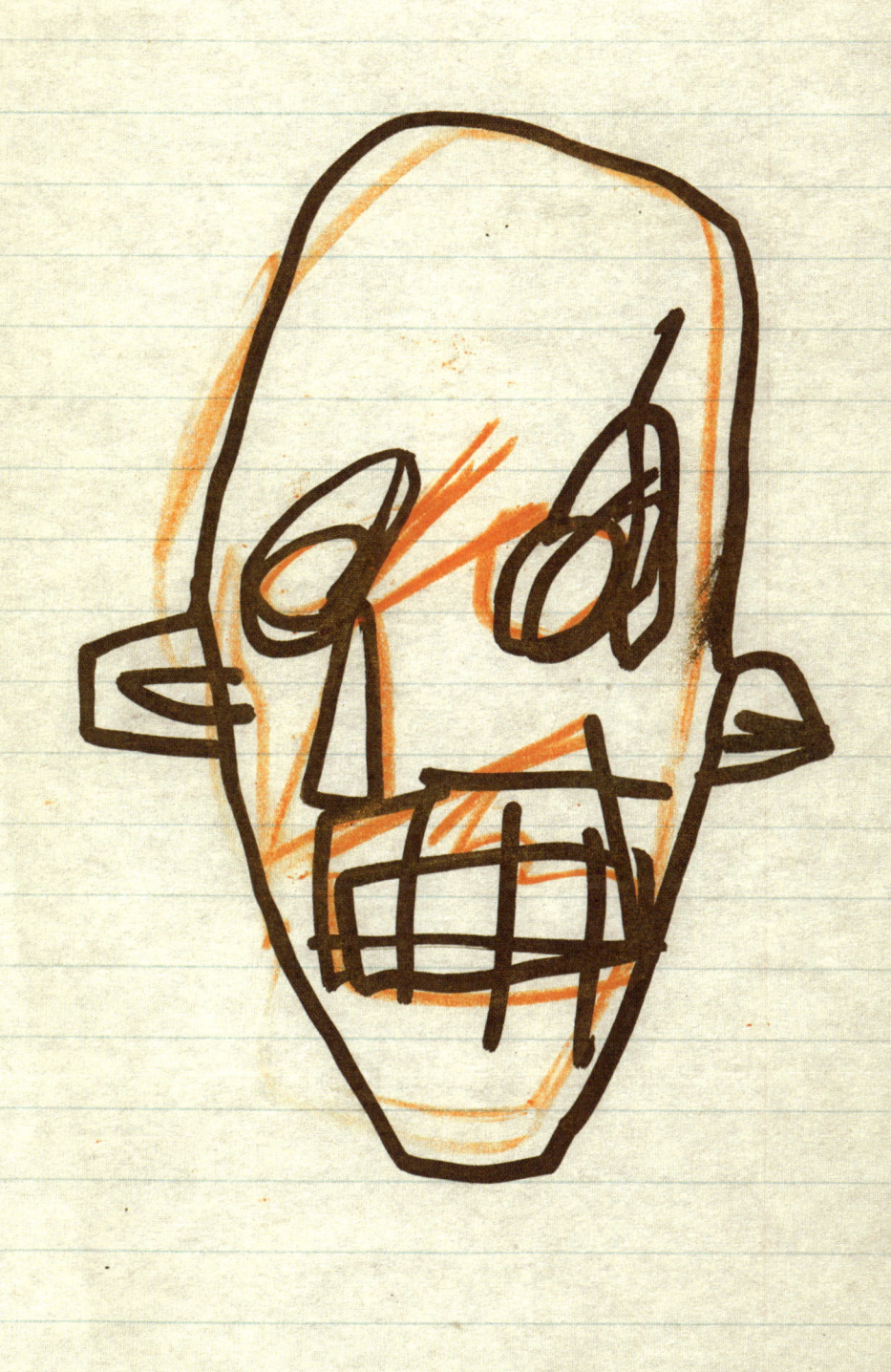

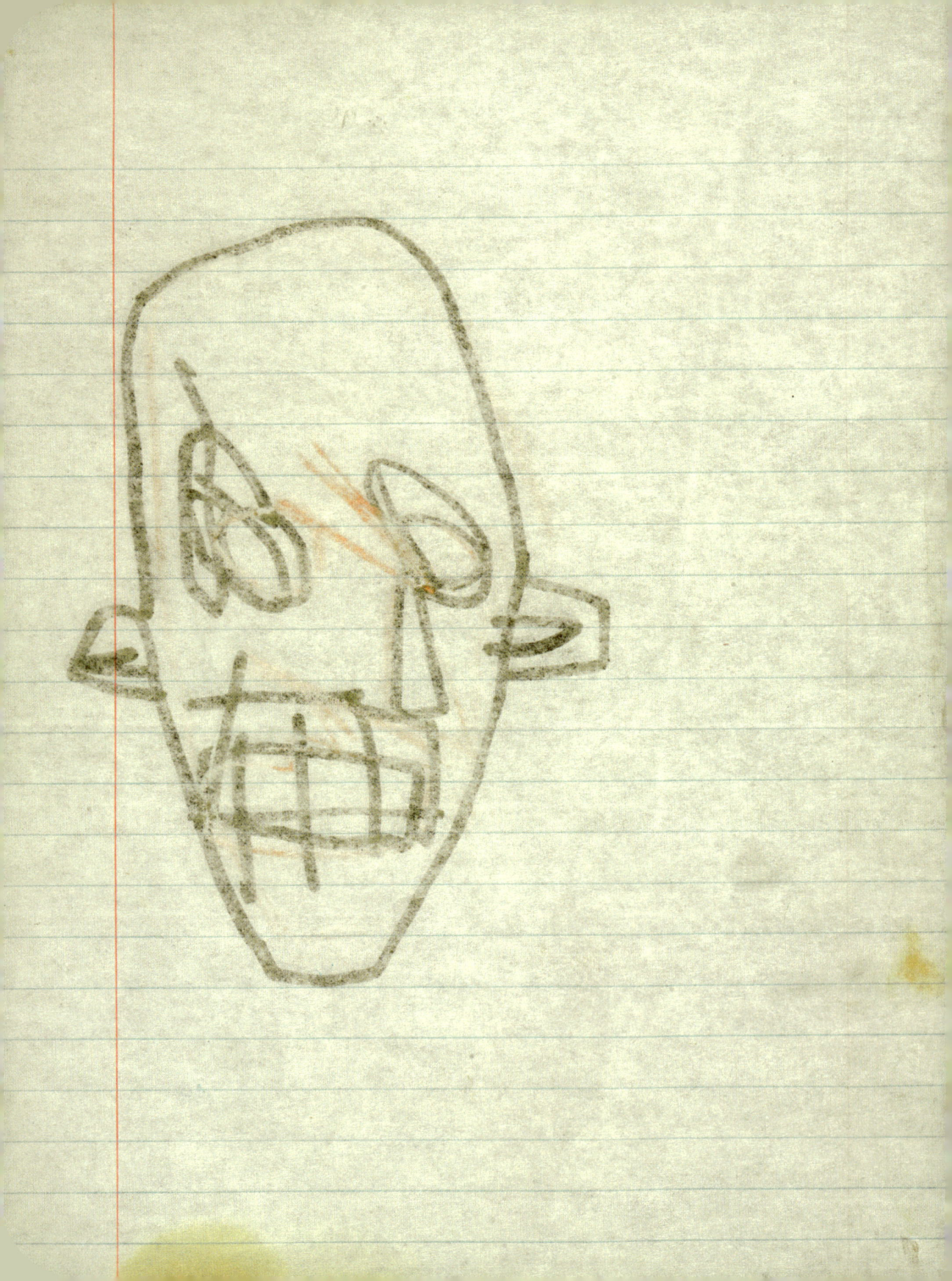

A QUICK TURN SWEATING TOO MUCH

LIGHT DISTURB

LIKE THE PY SYMBOL

SWEATING TOO MUCH

IS THAT A LIGHT?

SIMPLE BELLS

SWEATING TOO MUCH

THEY'LL SEE MY PAPERS WEARING AWAY IN MY FACE

FALSO

~~MINERALS IN LUGGAGE TAGS~~

A SOIL RICH IN SULPHUR

~~A BARREL~~

~~A PARRELEL~~

A CRESENT SUN

A DESIRED SEXUAL EFFECT A

A ROPE LADDER OF BEDSHEETS
A DESIRED SEXUAL EFFECT
LOW FUN ⟩ A MINIATURE STATE
A MOUNTING NUMBER / A QUICK TURN SWEATING TOO MUCH
LIGHT DISTURB / SWEATING TOO MUCH
IS THAT A LIGHT / FALSO
A SOIL RICH IN SULPHUR / PULL IN A DOG TO DRAW SANDPAPER
PUT HIM ON A MAT / CENSOR HIS HABITS —
TO BRING TO THE POINT OF SNAP-LOGIC TO TURN TO
THE CLOSEST AND OPEN THE AIR LOCK EXPIRING.
SIX OF US COURTING AN AMERICAN MADONNA ——

THE WORLD'S FOUR MAJOR

GRAIN, OIL AND IRON ORE

SIXTY BANKS

A GROUP OF MONEYMEN

SEAMY BLANC MORTARS

TO BRING HIM TO THE POINT/SNAP LOGIC/TO TURN TO THE
ONES CLOSEST/OPEN THE AIR LOCK/EXPIRING⟩

HOLMAN

751054B

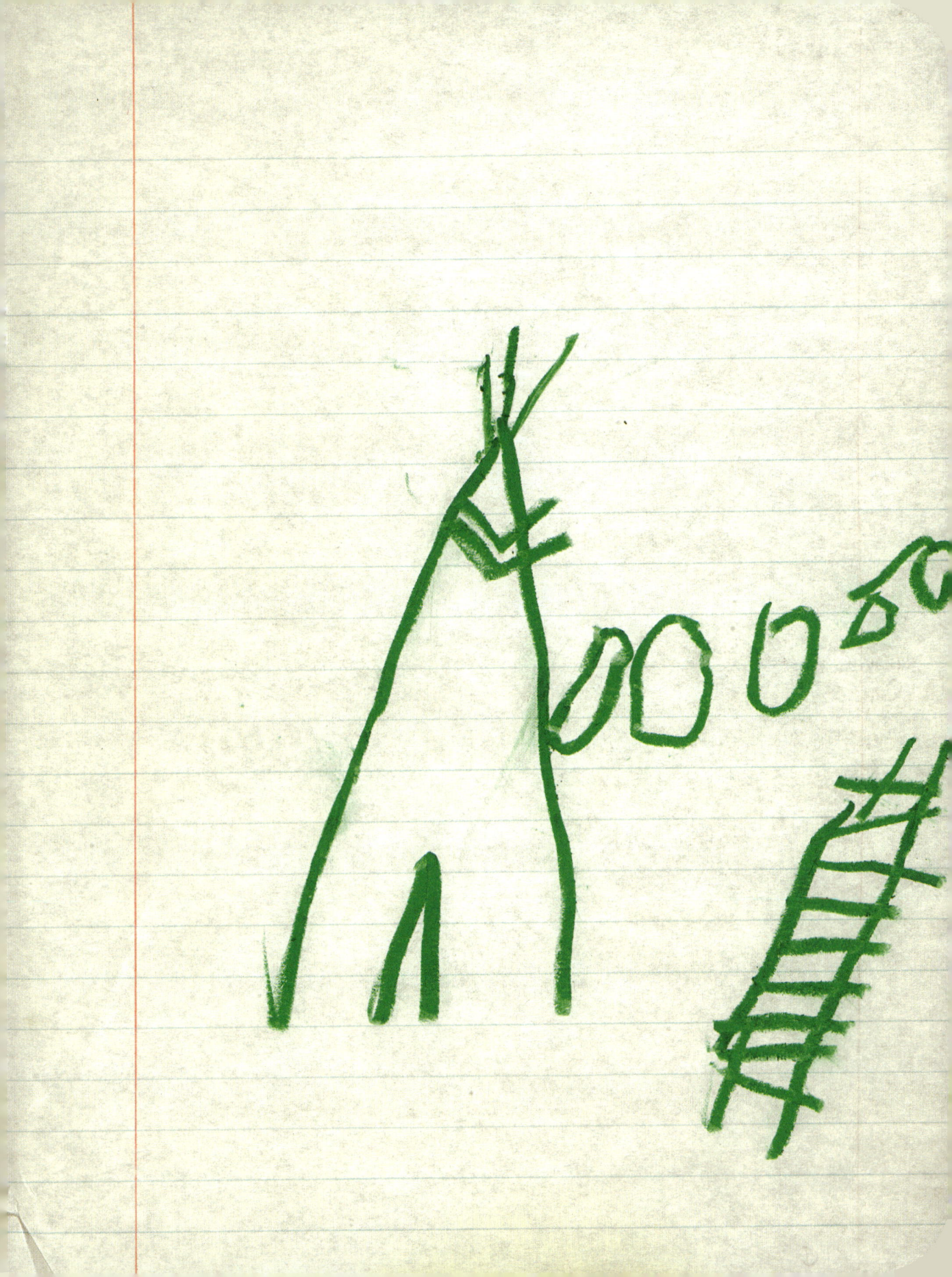

MARYANN.   228 3968

IT TOOK THE GUILT OF FOUR GENERATIONS
OF SWEATSHOP WORKER TO GAIN
ACCESS TO THE STATESMAN.

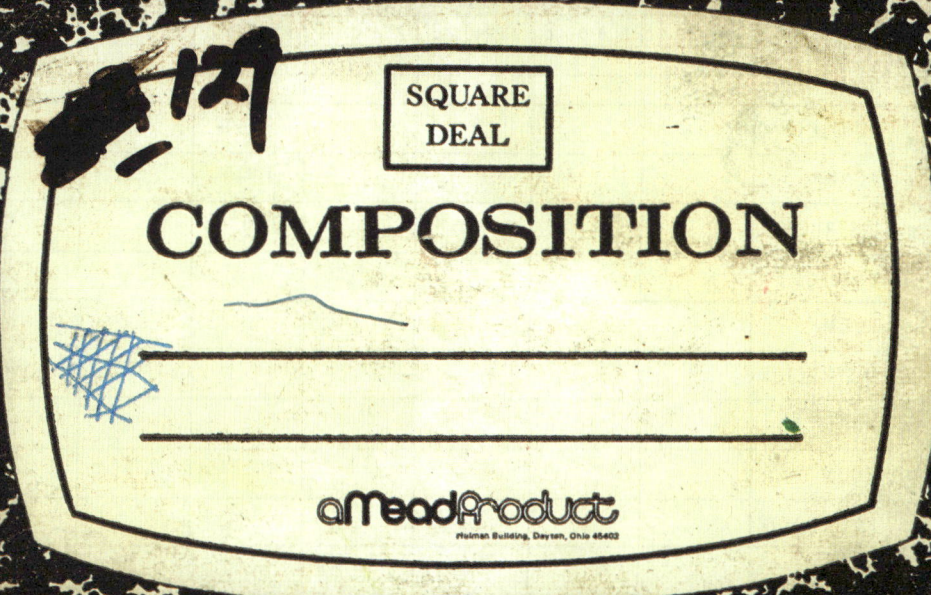

SQUARE
DEAL

COMPOSITION

aMeadProduct
Holman Building, Dayton, Ohio 45402

CLASS PROGRAM

NAME_____ ADDRESS_____

SCHOOL_____ CLASS_____

	TIME	FROM TO...	PERIOD 1	PERIOD 2	PERIOD 3	PERIOD 4	PERIOD 5	PERIOD 6	PERIOD 7	PERIOD 8
MONDAY	SUBJECT									
	ROOM									
	INSTRUCTOR									
TUESDAY	SUBJECT									
	ROOM									
	INSTRUCTOR									
WEDNESDAY	SUBJECT									
	ROOM									
	INSTRUCTOR									
THURSDAY	SUBJECT									
	ROOM									
	INSTRUCTOR									
FRIDAY	SUBJECT									
	ROOM									
	INSTRUCTOR									
SATURDAY	SUBJECT									
	ROOM									
	INSTRUCTOR									

No. 09-6120 • WIDE RULED with MARGIN

120 SHEETS • SIZE 9¾ IN. x 7½ IN.

SHE LOOKED HER THIRD EYE ACROSS THE PARLOR AT A SINSAE DIPLOMAT
FROZE UNDER PALM AT AN ESCAPIST RESORT ON THE BEACH
THRU THE WATER HER EYE BECAME A BEGGAR IN SPAIN
IN FRONT OF A TOURIST TRAP HER VOICE PARROTS A
SANDPAPER WHINE OVER TELEFONATA.

SLEEPING ON SIX TRAINS FLYING HOME WATCHING THE
WINGS SHAKE IS IT MY IMAGINATION BUT DO
THE BUILDINGS SHAKE FROM THE SUBWAY

THE TELEGRAPH OUTSIDE THE HOTEL LOOKS COLLAPSIBLE.

A CITIZENS MONOGRAM ON STRIKE PLACCARDS
FIRMLY BELIEVES BLOCKAGE
THE CALLUSES OF SURVIVAL—

A CRUCIFIX ON THE TOWER TRANSMITTING INTO 20,000
TELEVISIONS ~~IN~~ (CIRCA 1938) A GOLD DUBLOON ON
A MONKEY HEAD HYSTERIA TAMED BY A NATURAL
ORDER ~~OF QUENCHING SPIRITS~~
WATERTOWERS / HIGH·RISE
NO VACANCY ON AND OFF CRUSTY MENOSTAFF
RECIEVER NODDING PULLED BACK PLUGS—
OFF EAR PAUSE IRRIDESCENCE QUENCHING
BRICK FEAR OF THE TOWER
20 FIRE ESCAPES ERECTED ON THE SAME DAY
FALL PARRELEL·

LITTLE GLASS OFFICES SHATTERING OFF THE RUNWAY.

1000 YEAR OLD STREET

STOPPED IN TRANSIT SEVEN TIMES

A CRUCIFIX ON A TOWER TRANSMITTING INTO
20000 TELEVISIONS CIRCA 1938
GOLD DUBLOON ON A MONKEY HEAD HYSTERIA
TAMED BY NATURAL ORDER
A TURN OF THE HEAD FINGERS ON A KNOB
SMILING TOO MUCH
JUST A THIEF COLLABORATING

SHE LOOKED HER THIRD EYE AT A SINSAE DIPLOMAT
ACROSS THE PARLOR FROZE UNDER PALM
AT A BEACH RESORT

STILL BREAST·FEEDS HER BABY ALL WITH TEETH

COLORS WITH NUMBERS ON THE BACK
BROOMING INTO MEZZO/ASPURIA

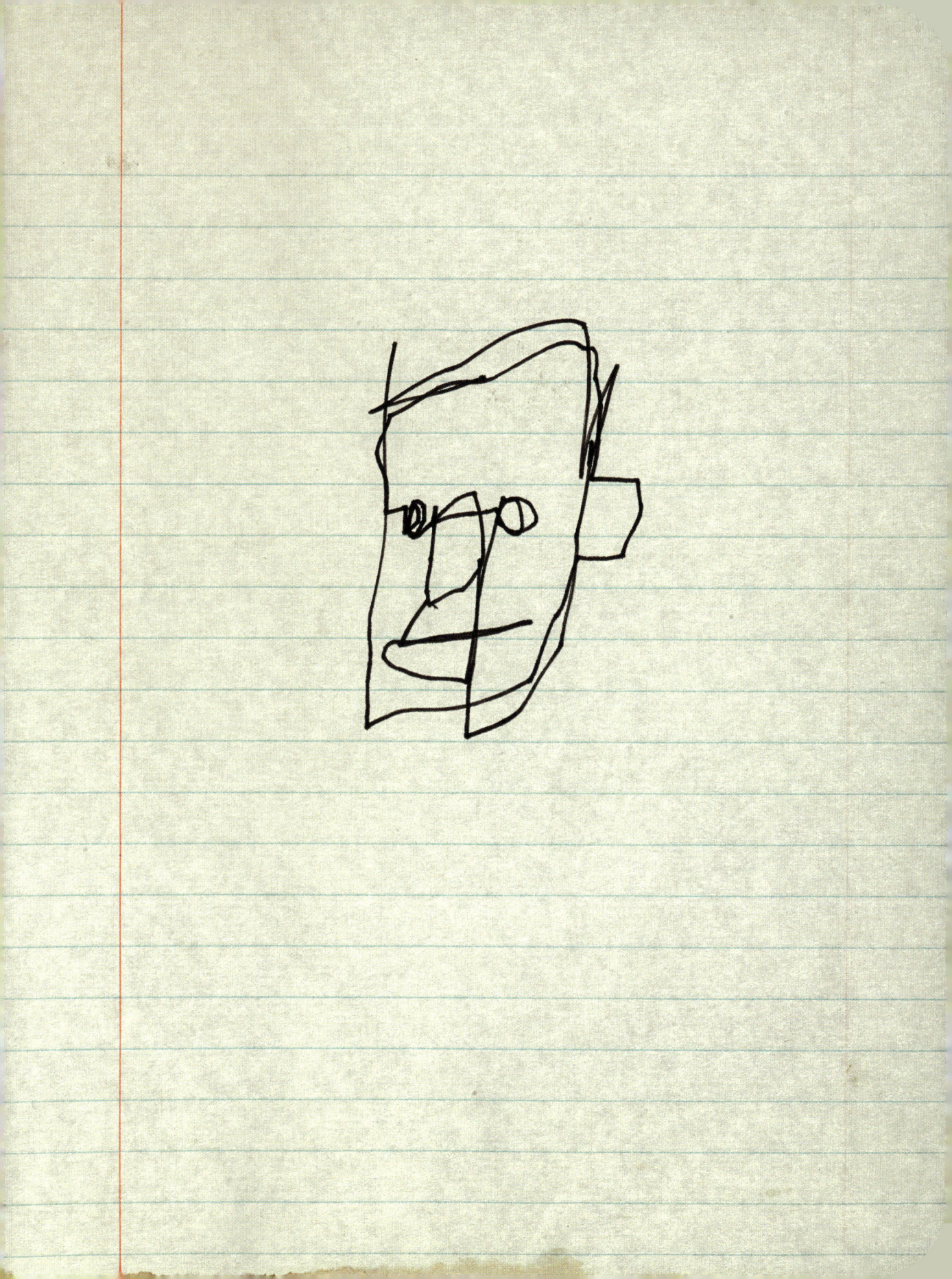

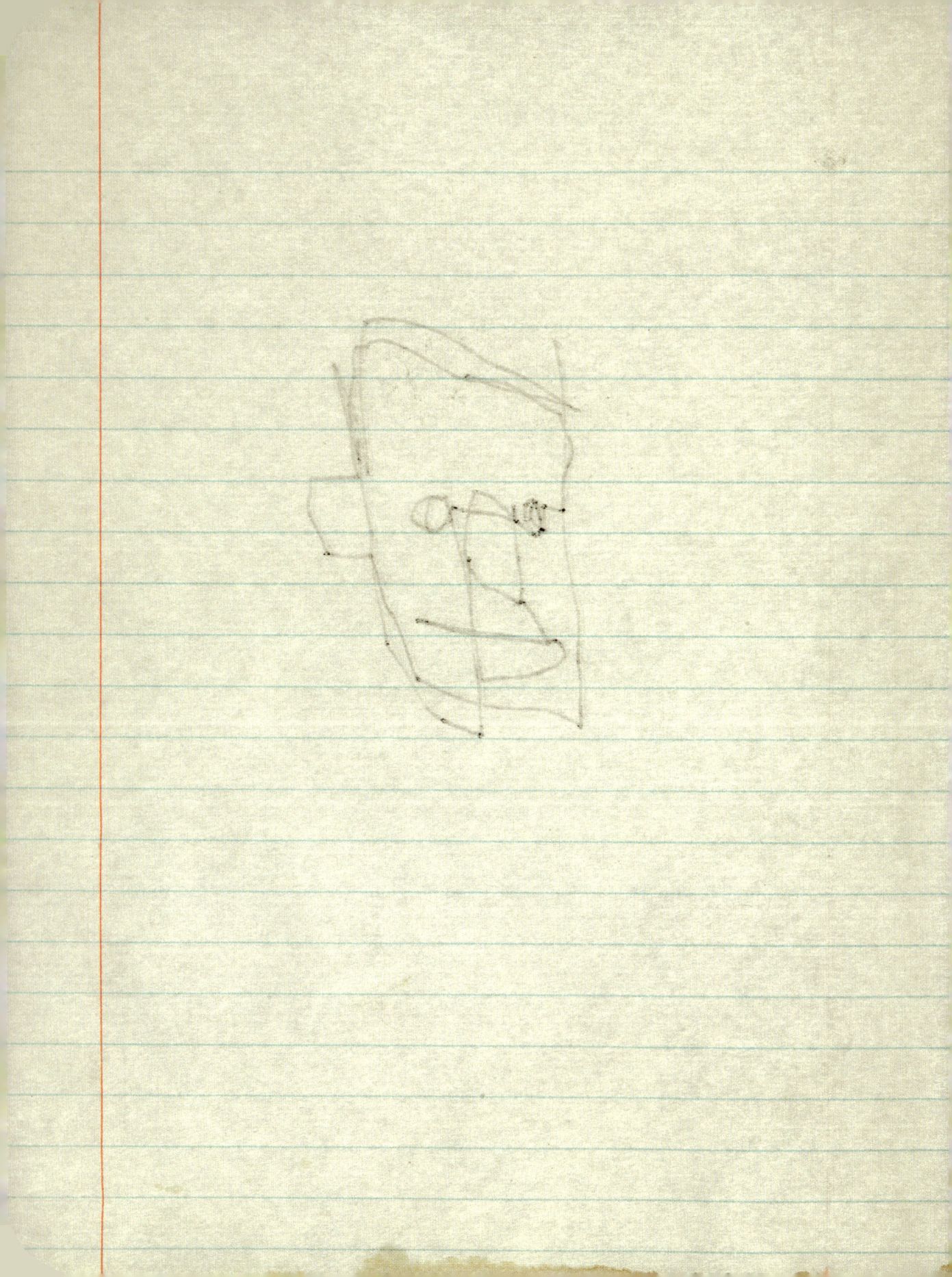

A SOIL RICH IN ⚡ SULPHUR—FALSO/ A QUICK TURN
SWEATING TOO MUCH. —LIKE THE PY SYMBOL
IS THAT A LIGHT? SWEATING TOO MUCH/FALSO.

CRUCIFIX TRANSMITTING INTO 20,000 TELEVISIONS
CIRCA 1938)
MONKEY HEAD HYSTERIA TAMED BY A NATURAL ORDER
SMILING TOO MUCH A THIEF COLLABORATING

SHE LOOKED HER THIRD EYE ACROSS THE
PARLOR AT A SINSAE DIPLOMAT FROZE
UNDER PALM AT AN ESCAPIST RESORT
ON THE BEACH.

THRU THE WATER HER EYE BECOMES A BEGGAR
IN SPAIN.

IS IT MY ɣ IMAGINATION OR DOES THE BUILDING
SHAKE

TELEGRAPH OUTSIDE THE HOTEL LOOKS COLLAPSES—

SO SUFFERING THE WHOLE THING ABOUT HIS FOOT
STILL BREAST FED AFTER TEETH.
STILL BREAST FED/SO SUFFERING
A SOIL RICH IN SULPHUR > FALSO
SWEATING TOO MUCH
IS THAT A LIGHT?

THE AREA CODE OF ST. LOUIS ✦ PRIOR TO THE ASSASINATION.

FLICK OF THE WRISK

JAPANESE ARCHITECHTS

AREA CODE OF ST. LOUIS

A MARATHON SUICIDE CIRCLE GETS ON 20 COVERS IN 24 HOURS

ALL BARKING

LIVING COLOR

NO TREBLE

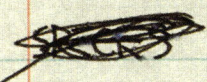

30 LOGS FOR A BAG OF SUGAR SCREAMS THE MERCHANT
2 ACCOMPLICES DRAG IN SOME CARROTS AND WIPE THEM
WITH KEROSENE TO STRIP THE SKINS.

A BARLEY RUN ON CHARTER AIRLINE CAUSE $\cancel{4}$ CHEMICAL
FUSION 2 SOURCES

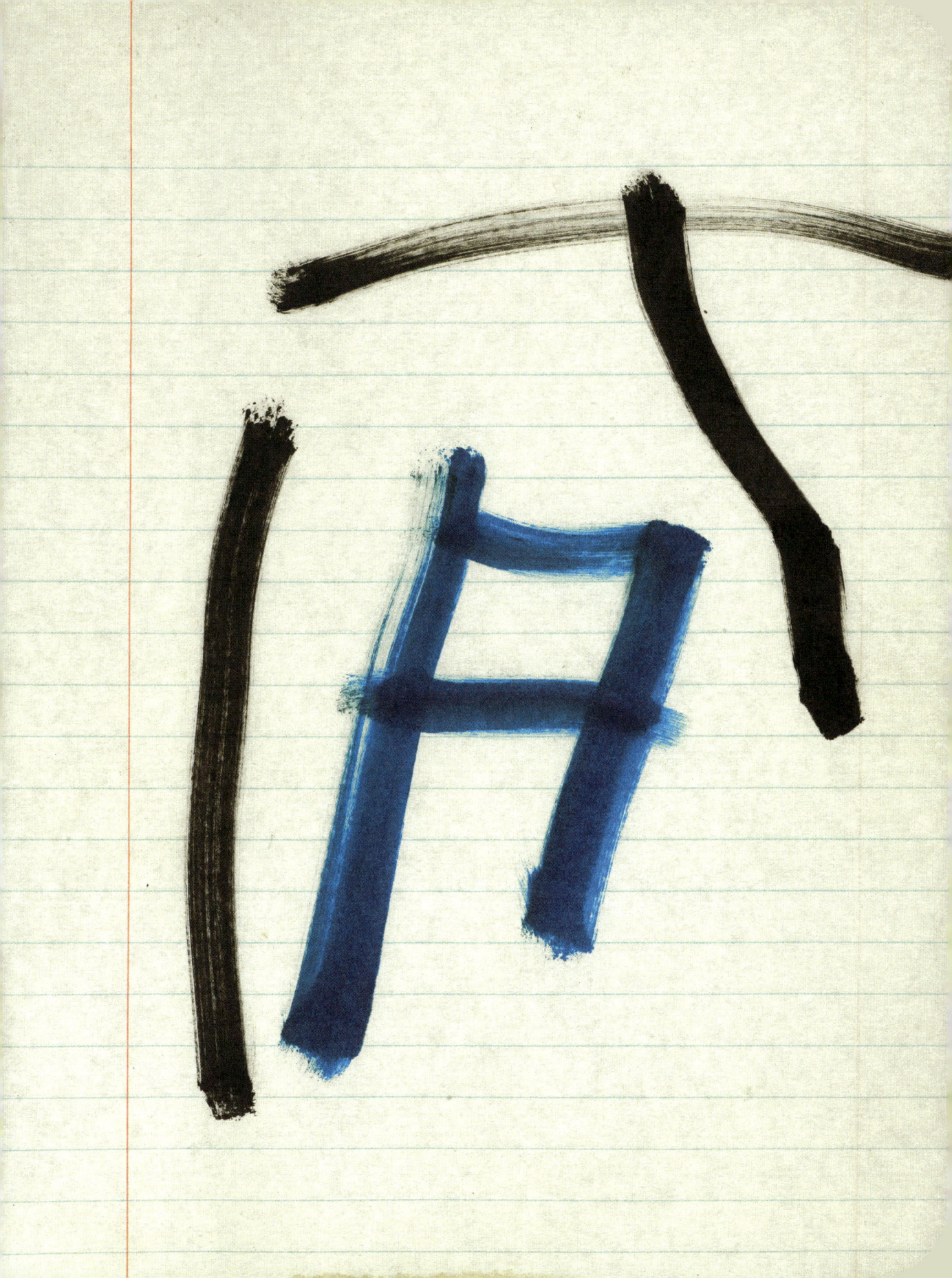

BABY SAY

BABY SAY

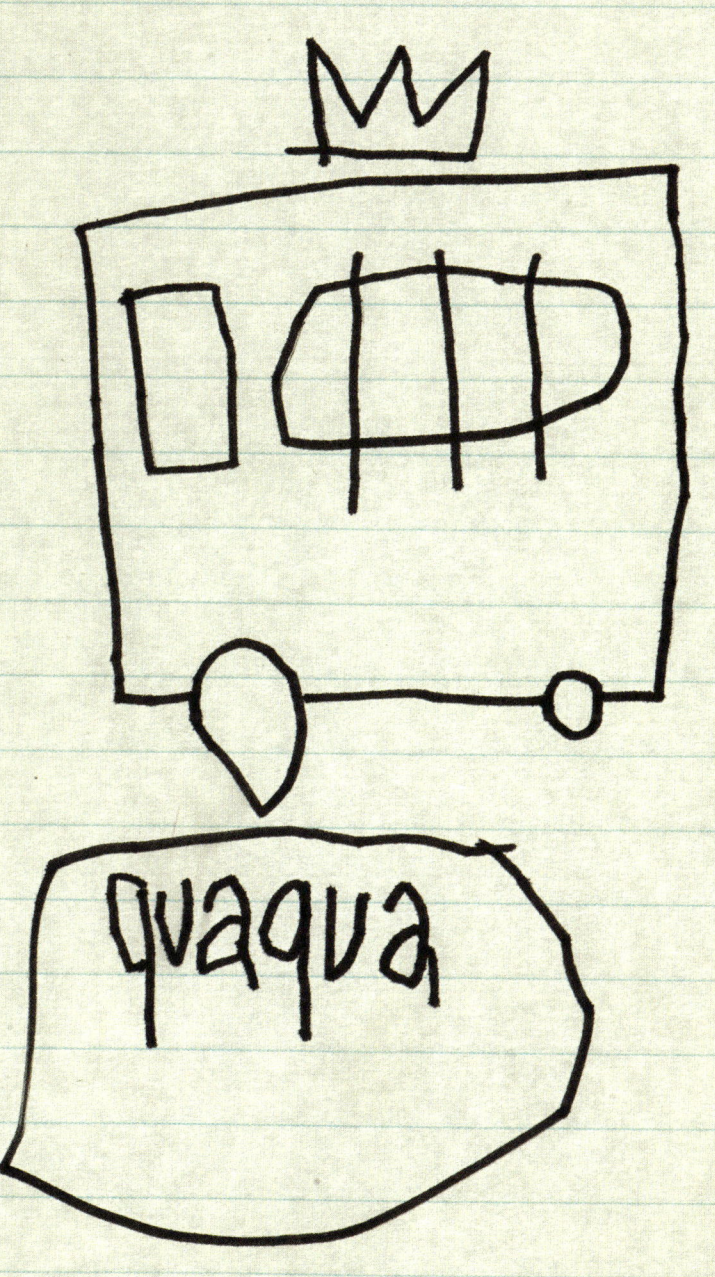

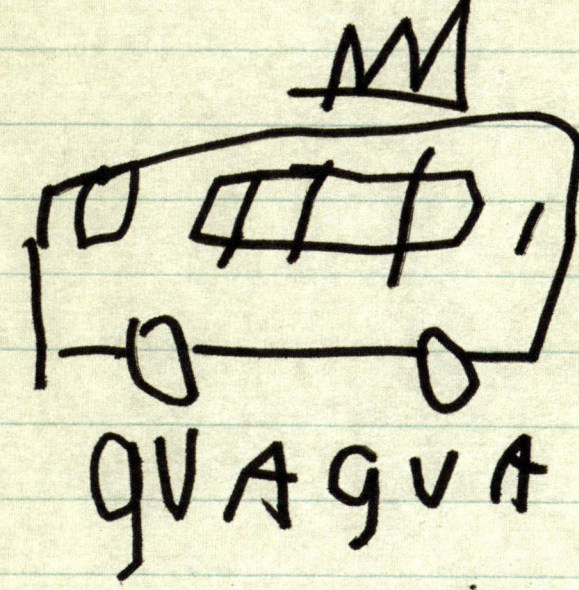

GUAGUA

THE DOG DIED

A RIGHT-WING GROUP ON TELEVISION

THE TEXT FOR MECHAN

A TEXT ON TRANSLATING

HOME WORKBENCH

SURVEILENCE UNDERTONES

VERN AS THE PRESIDENT.

SECRET SERVICE MAN INTRODUCES THE PRESIDENT OF

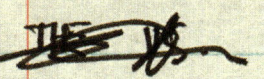

PSYCHIATRIT. ARTO
THE PRESIDENT OF WECON· VERN
BODYGUARD· JEFFERY.
SECRETARY·

CHALK MARK CAUSES ACCIDENT.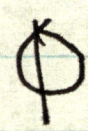

MARY

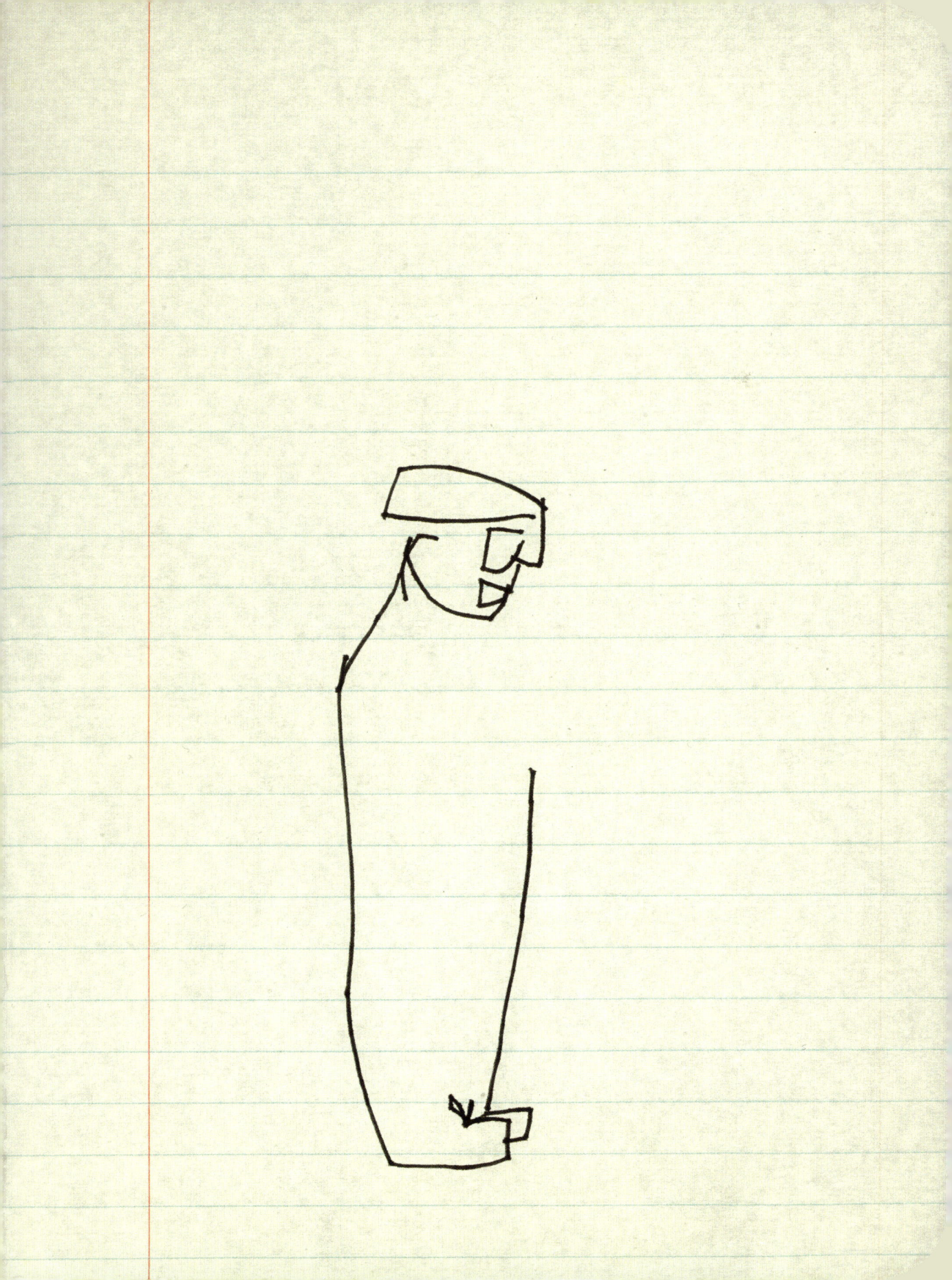

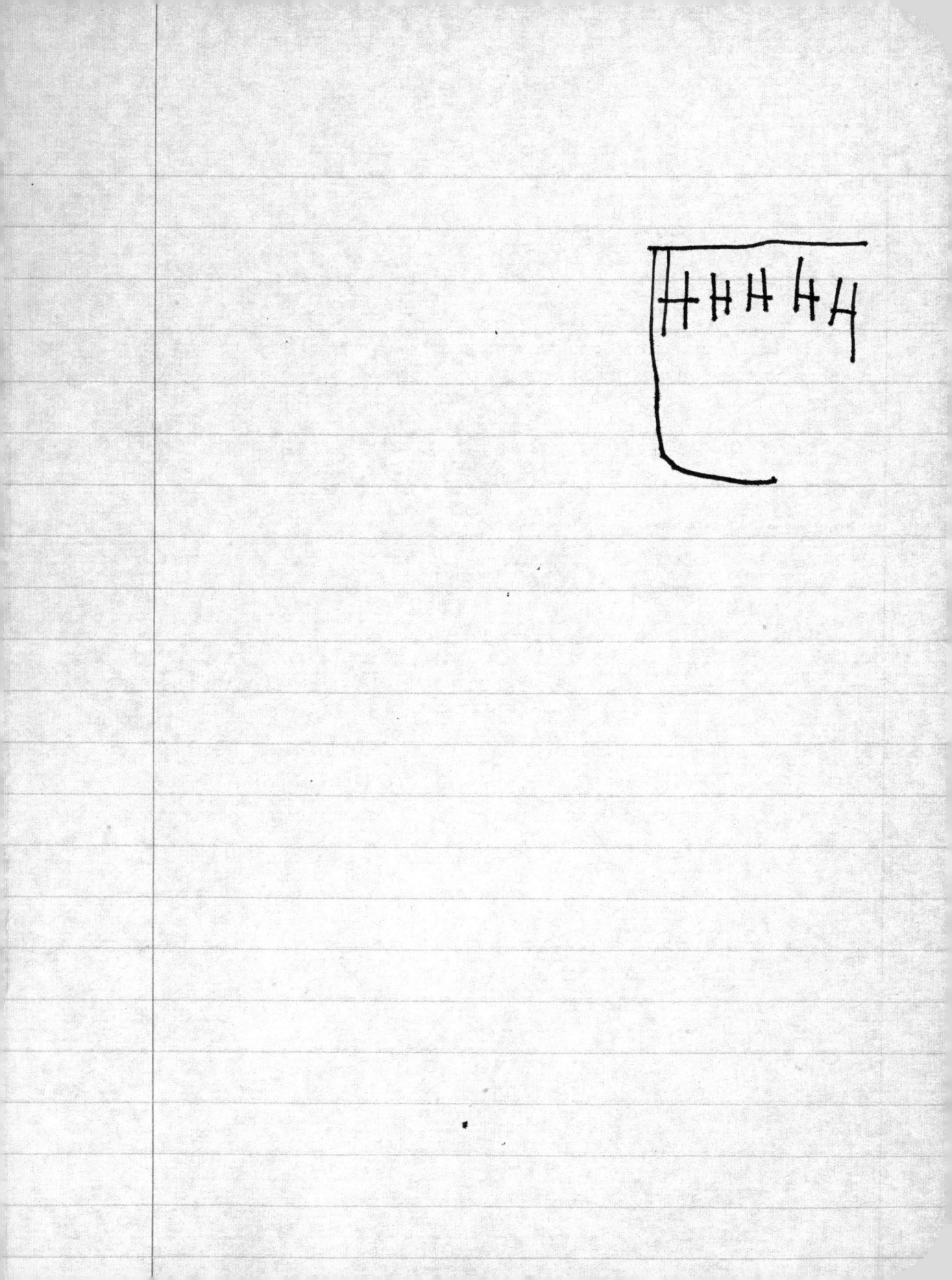

SOMETIME

GET TO THIS FORK IN THE ROAD.

MARc Francis 431 - 7304

CLASS PROGRAM

NAME_____ ADDRESS_____

SCHOOL_____ CLASS_____

TIME	FROM TO…	PERIOD 1	PERIOD 2	PERIOD 3	PERIOD 4	PERIOD 5	PERIOD 6	PERIOD 7	PERIOD 8
MONDAY SUBJECT									
ROOM									
INSTRUCTOR									
TUESDAY SUBJECT									
ROOM									
INSTRUCTOR									
WEDNESDAY SUBJECT									
ROOM									
INSTRUCTOR									
THURSDAY SUBJECT									
ROOM									
INSTRUCTOR									
FRIDAY SUBJECT									
ROOM									
INSTRUCTOR									
SATURDAY SUBJECT									
ROOM									
INSTRUCTOR									

Mead
60 Sheets
9¾ in x 7½ in
24.7 cm x 19.0 cm
Wide Ruled
09-4160   The Mead Corporation, Dayton, Ohio 45463

MARK TWAIN

ART

BALTIC AVE ™

©

MONOPOLY HAT ©

HAT

MONOPOLY

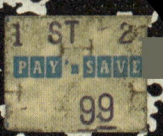

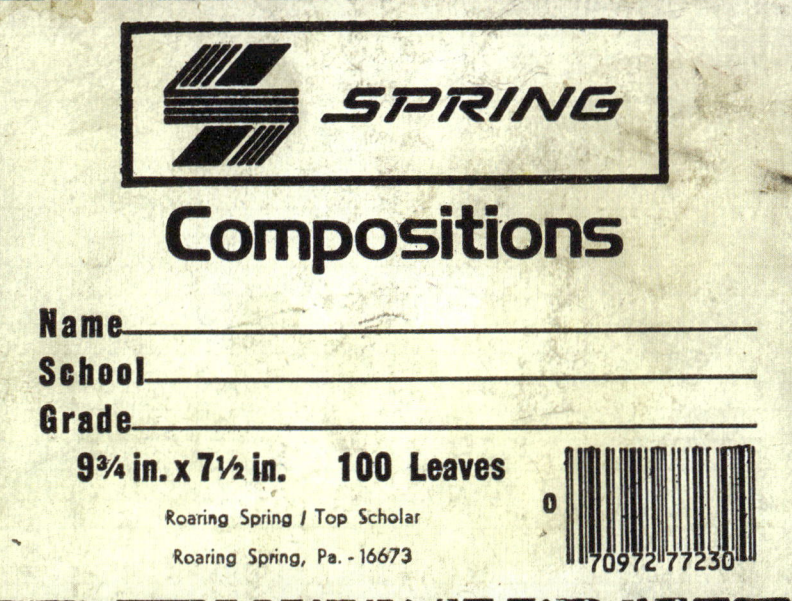

Spring

Compositions

Name_____

School_____

Grade_____

9¾ in. x 7½ in.   **100 Leaves**

Roaring Spring / Top Scholar

Roaring Spring, Pa. - 16673

0 70972 77230

CHRIS JOHNSON
272 6572

Daniel
923 5767

310 W. 56 PH # D
ANN
661 7778.

CLASS PROGRAM

Date | | | |

Family Name			Given Name					Class		Room	
	MON.	RM.	TUES.	RM.	WED.	RM.	THURS.	RM.	FRI.	RM.		
1												
2												
3												
4												
5												
6												
7												
8												
9												
10												
11												
12												

NAME_____ ADDRESS_____

RALF "PENCK"
(411) 24.90.433

DON'T LOOK AT TH

~~SAUNAKEANNA~~

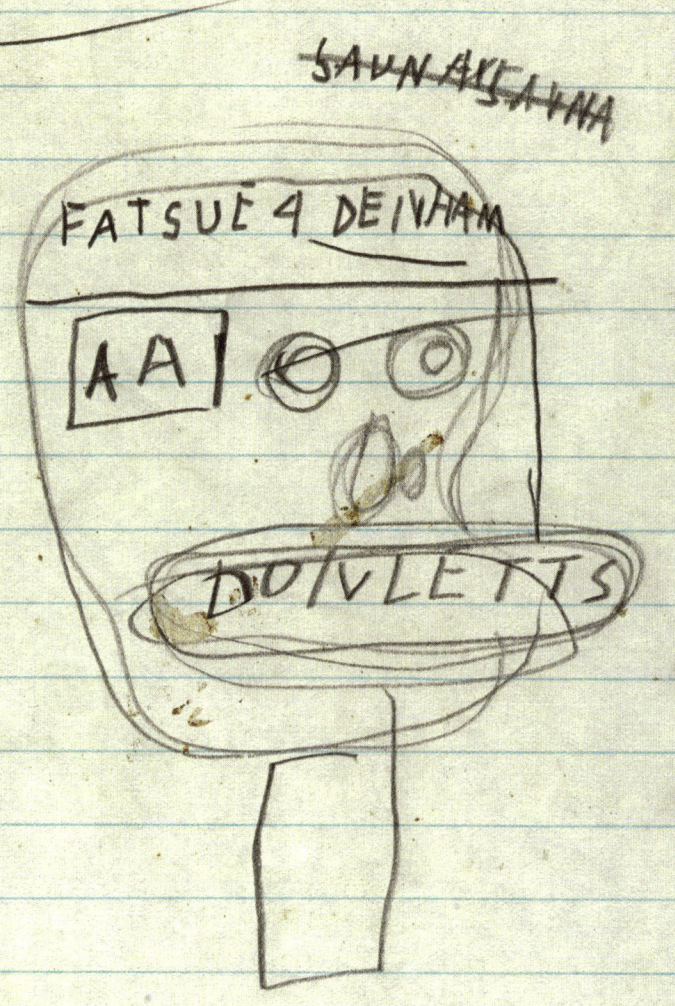

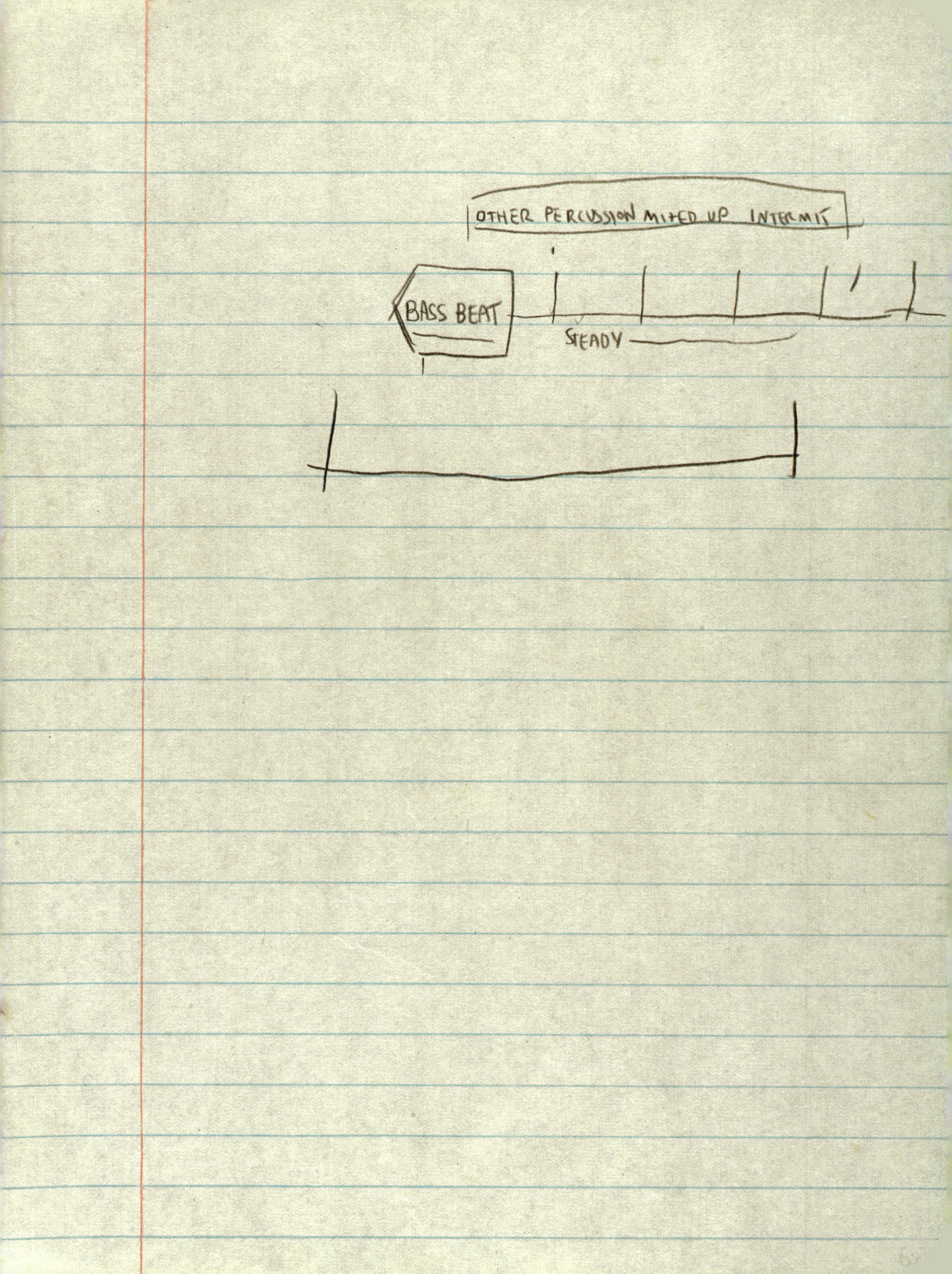

OTHER PERCUSSION MIXED UP INTERMIT

BASS BEAT

STEADY

A DARK ROOM / SOUND OF RINGING PHONE LIGHT ON PHONE FLASHES

7 RINGS SILENCE / SHOT OF TELEVISION STATIC / LIGHT COMING

FROM BATHROOM ON PERSON / NO MOVEMENT / PHONE RINGS

A GAIN PERSON LOOKS OUT BLINDS / DARK OUTSIDE

PUTS ON LIGHT GOES TO PHONE STOPS RINGING —

GOES DOWNSTAIRS NUDE DRINKS A GLASS OF SEVEN·UP

COMES BACK UPSTAIRS PHONE RINGS PICKS IT UP. —

(SHOTS OF FULL ASHTRAYS, DRUG PARAPHANAIL(A) —

(HI, I JUST WOKE UP OK I'LL BE THERE IN A WHILE)

PUTS ON AN UBEAT CALYPSO / SOCA DANCES AROUND TO WAKE UP

PUTS ON JAZZ AND TAKES A SHOWER —

TAXI TO SPANISH RESTARAUNT —

CONVERSATION —

LOUIS THE 14TH + RIBBONS —

VILLAGE GREEN + GHOSTS UNDISCOVERED DEATH —

FLIRTATION WITH WAITRESS —

CHRISTMAS TALK —

GAVIN: YOU MUST TRY THE PIG EARS (FABULOUS!) THIS IS MY

FRIEND SOPHIE

SOPHIE: ~~YOU MUST~~   I LOVE THE PAINTING IN THE BACK ROOM

AT THE GALLERY SOME OF MY ^YOUR PAINTINGS I HATE BUT

I WOULD DO A LOT OF THINGS FOF THIS ONE.

GAVIN:

LOUIS THE FOURTEENTH HAD THIS THING FOR RIBBONS

I CAN SEE HIM ROLLING DOWN VERSAILIE

THIS LITTLE SHOE WITH THIS BIG RIBBON

WOMAN: THAT WAS JUST TO HELP THE RIBBON INDUSTRY ALL THE COURT

    WORE, ALL EUROPE + —

HE WAS PASTY WHITE +

NO HE WAS SWARTHY, DARK AND SEXY —

NO HE WAS PASTY WHITE x —

_____

YUCK, SPANISH BRANDY —

RUSSIAN BRANDY + —

A WALK DOWN THE STREET —

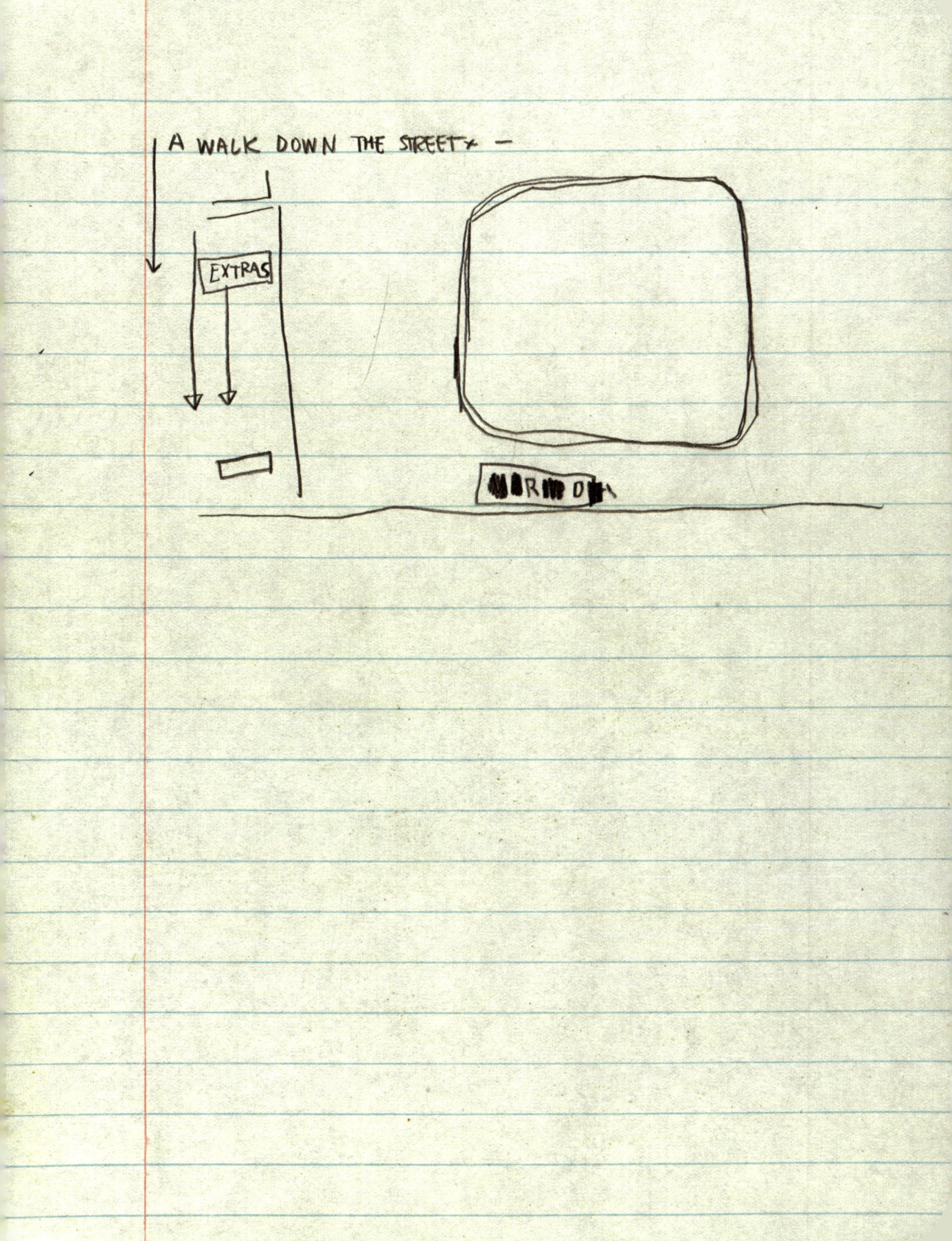

EXTRAS

MIRROR

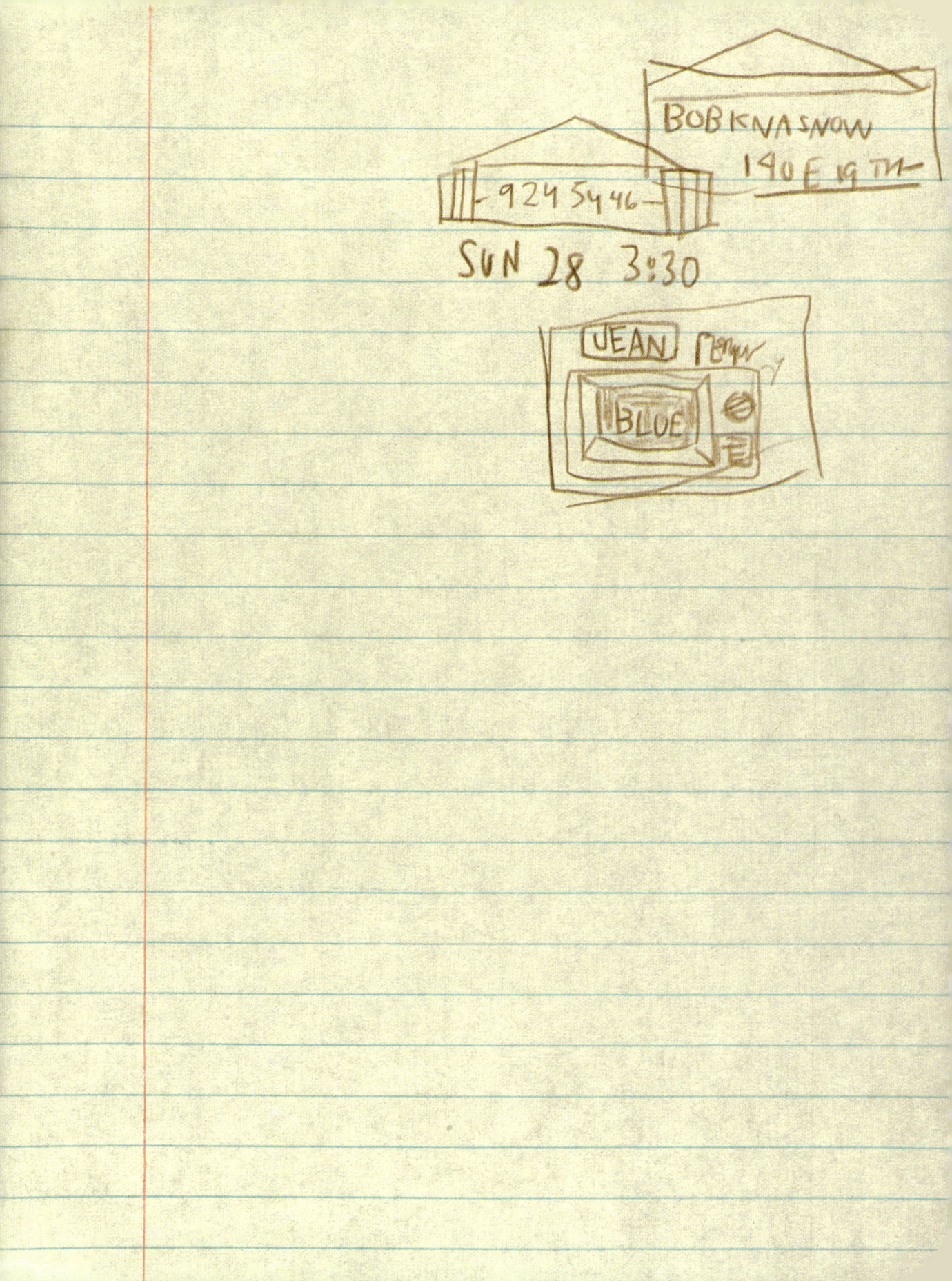

BOB KNASNOW
190 E 19TH

9245446

SUN 28 3:30

JEAN rogers

BLUE

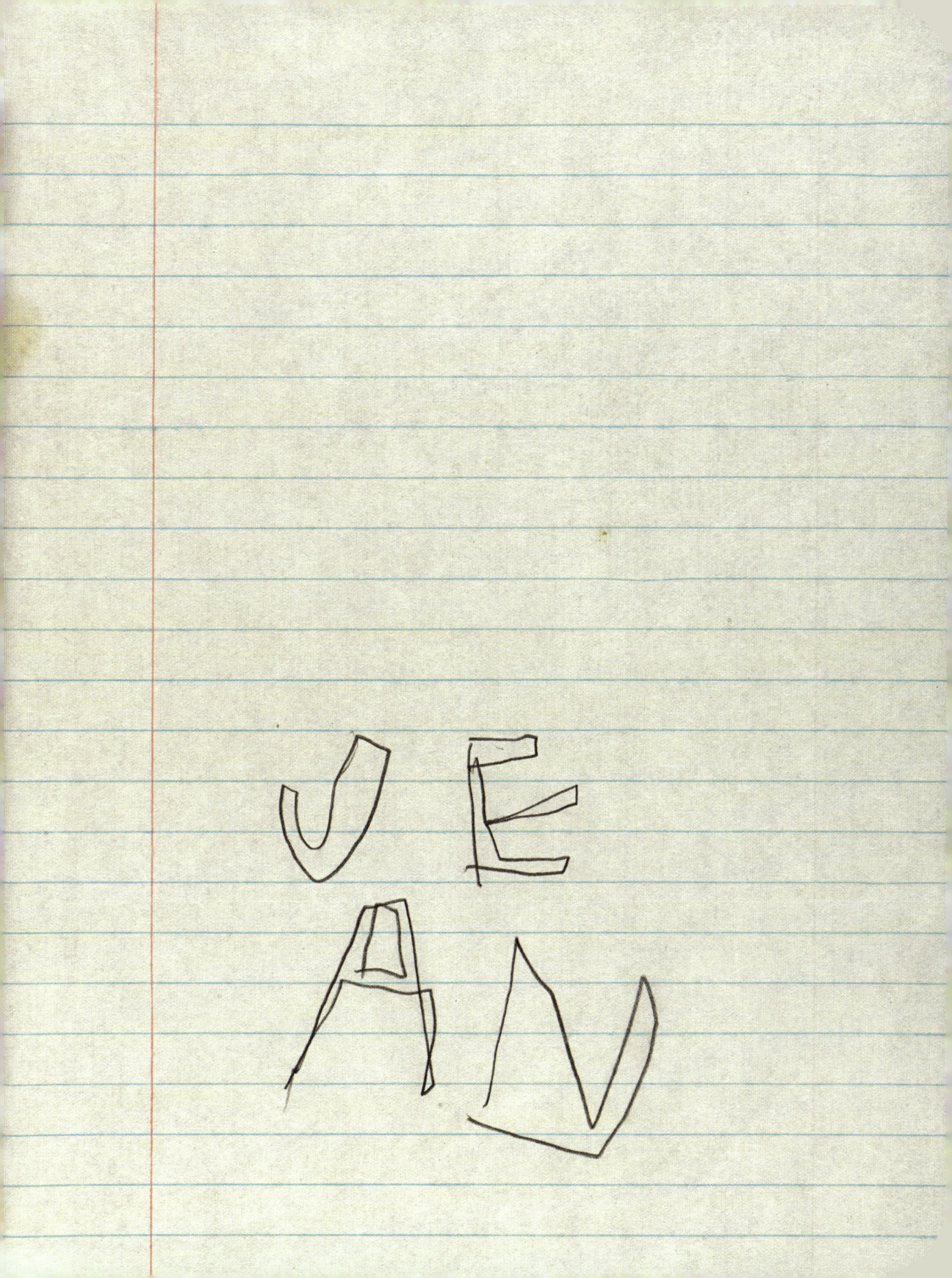

9685267 DONCETTS-

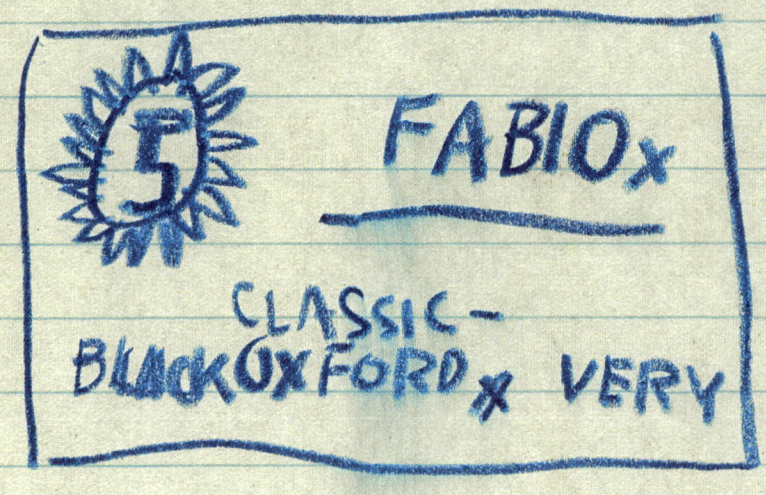

IN STOCKHOLM THEY HAVE THIER ROACHES IN A ZOO.

~~SHE TOLD~~

A COMBINATION OF WORRY AND THOUGHT—

A FOURTEEN YEAR OLD SWEDE IN NEW YORK
1951.— GOES TO BIRDLAND AND ·BEGS
TO BE PHOTOGRAPHED WITH CHARLIE FUCKING—
BIRD PARKER — SHE SHRUGS HIM OFF
~~CHARLIE PARKER RETURN~~

~~CHARLIE BUY HIM ALL HIS~~
CHARLIE MAKES HIM BUY ALL HIS RECORDS—

SWEDISH CHOCOLATE SOLDIERS—

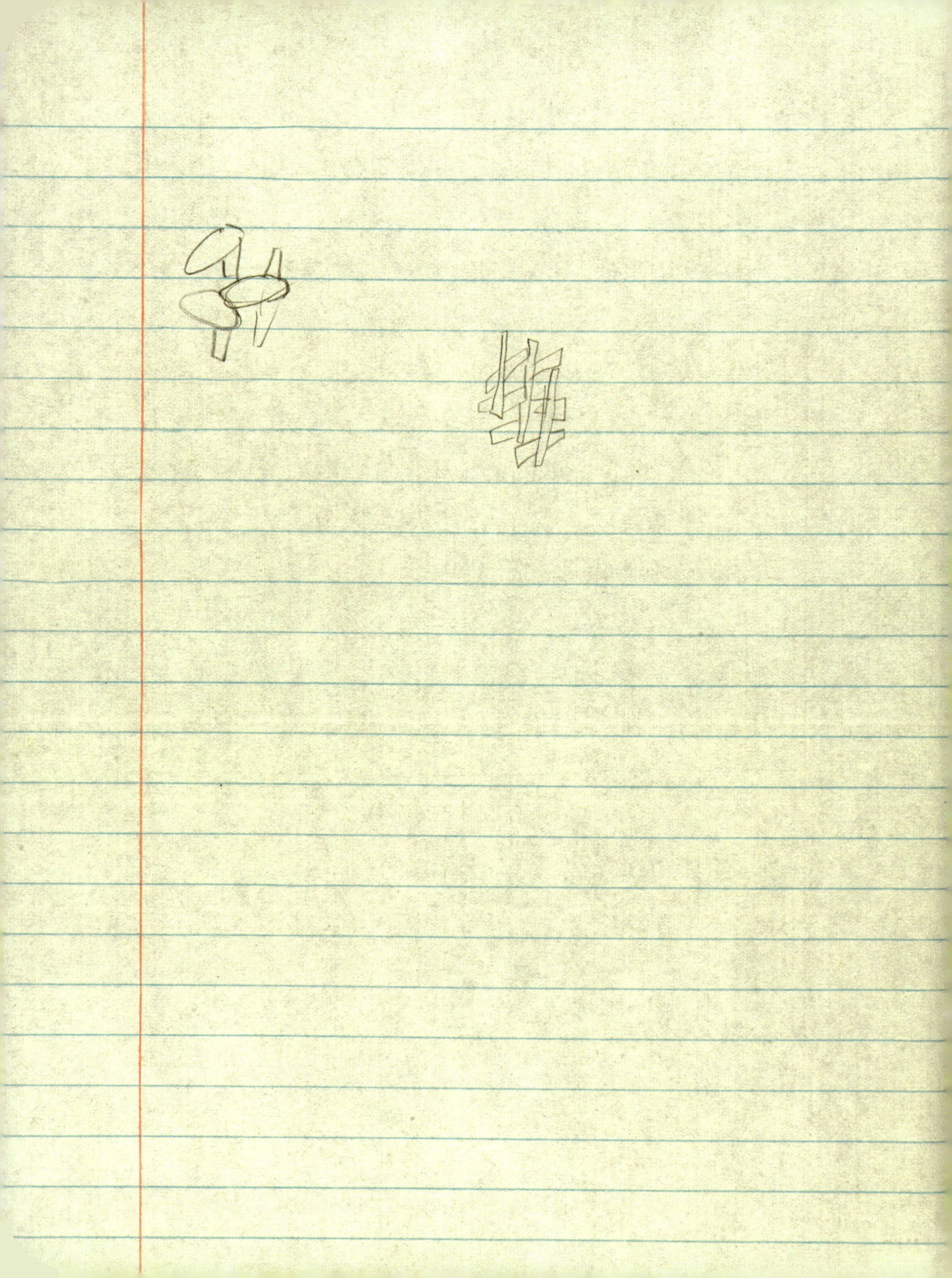

USEFUL INFORMATION

LIQUID MEASURE

4 gills (gi.) = 1 pint (pt.)
2 pints = 1 quart (qt.)
4 quarts = 1 gallon (gal.) (231 cu. in.)
31½ gallons = 1 barrel (bbl.)
2 barrels = 1 hogshead (hhd.)
1 cubic foot of water = 7.48 gallons
1 cubic foot of water weighs approximately 62½ pounds.

CUBIC MEASURE

1728 cubic inches (cu. in.) = 1 cubic foot (cu. ft.)
27 cubic feet = 1 cubic yard (cu yd.)
16 cubic feet = 1 cord foot of wood
128 cubic feet or 8 cord feet = 1 cord of wood

NOTE:—A cord of wood is equivalent to a pile 8 feet long, 4 feet wide, and 4 feet high.

24¾ cubic feet = 1 perch (P.)

NOTE:—A perch of stone or brick is equivalent to a section 16½ feet long, 1½ feet wide, and 1 foot high. The unit is sometimes understood to mean 16½ cubic feet and sometimes 25 cubic feet.

40 cubic feet = 1 measurement ton, U. S. Shipping
42 cubic feet = 1 ton British Shipping

40 feet of round timber, or 50 feet of hewn timber = 1 ton or load

AVOIRDUPOIS WEIGHT

(Used in weighing all articles except drugs, gold, silver and precious stones)

27-11/32 grains (gr.) = 1 dram (dr.)
16 drams (437½ grs.) = 1 ounce (oz.)
16 ounces (7000 grs.) = 1 pound (lb.)
25 pounds = 1 quarter (qr.)
4 quarters or 100 pounds = 1 hundred-weight (cwt.)
2000 pounds or 20 hundredweight = 1 ton (T.)

NOTE:—The ton and hundredweight above given are those in common use in the United States.

2240 pounds = 1 long ton (L. T.)
13¼ cubic feet of air weighs = 1 pound

NOTE:—The grain has the same value in the Avoirdupois, Apothecaries' and Trey systems.

MISCELLANEOUS

12 units = 1 dozen
12 dozen = 1 gross
12 gross = 1 great gross
20 units = 1 score
4 inches = 1 hand
Diameter of circle x 3.1416 = circumference
Circumference of circle x .3183 = diameter
Diameter of circle squared x .7854 = area

Atmospheric pressure is 14.7 lbs. per square inch at sea level.

SQUARE MEASURE

144 square inches = 1 square foot (sq. ft.)
9 square feet = 1 square yard (sq. yd.)
30¼ square yards or 272¼ square feet = 1 square rod or 1 perch
40 square rods = 1 rood (R.)
160 square rods = 1 acre (A.)
640 acres = 1 square mile (sq. mi.)

A square having an area of 1 acre, measures 208.71 feet on each side.

1 township = 36 sections each 1 mile square
1 section = 640 acres
¼ section = ½ mile square or 160 acres
⅛ section = ½ mile long and ¼ mile wide or 80 acres
1 acre = 4840 square yards
1 acre = a lot 208.71 feet square

LINEAR MEASURE

1/12 inch = 1 line
12 inches = 1 foot (ft.)
3 feet = 1 yard (yd.)
5½ yards or 16½ feet = 1 rod (rd.) or pole
40 rods (660 f[illegible]t) = 1 furlong fur.)
320 rods (5280 feet or 8 furlongs) = 1 statute mile (m.)
3 miles = 1 league
6 feet = 1 fathom
120 fathoms = 1 cable-length
7⅓ cables = 1 statute mile
5280 feet = 1 statute mile
6080.2 feet = 1 geographical or nautical mile
1 geographical mile = 1.15155 statute mile
60 geographical miles = 1 degree longitude at equator
360 degrees = circumference of earth at equator

CIRCULAR MEASURE

60 seconds (") = 1 minute (')
60 minutes = 1 degree (°)
90 degrees = 1 quadrant
360 degrees = 1 circumference

A degree of the earth's surface on a meridian equals approximately 69 miles.

APOTHECARIES' FLUID MEASURE

60 minims = 1 fluid dram
8 fluid drams = 1 fluid ounce
16 fluid ounces = 1 pint
8 pints = 1 gallon

MULTIPLICATION TABLE

1	2	3	4	5	6	7	8	9	10	11	12
2	4	6	8	10	12	14	16	18	20	22	24
3	6	9	12	15	18	21	24	27	30	33	36
4	8	12	16	20	24	28	32	36	40	44	48
5	10	15	20	25	30	35	40	45	50	55	60
6	12	18	24	30	36	42	48	54	60	66	72
7	14	21	28	35	42	49	56	63	70	77	84
8	16	24	32	40	48	56	64	72	80	88	96
9	18	27	36	45	54	63	72	81	90	99	108
10	20	30	40	50	60	70	80	90	100	110	120
11	22	33	44	55	66	77	88	99	110	121	132
12	24	36	48	60	72	84	96	108	120	132	144

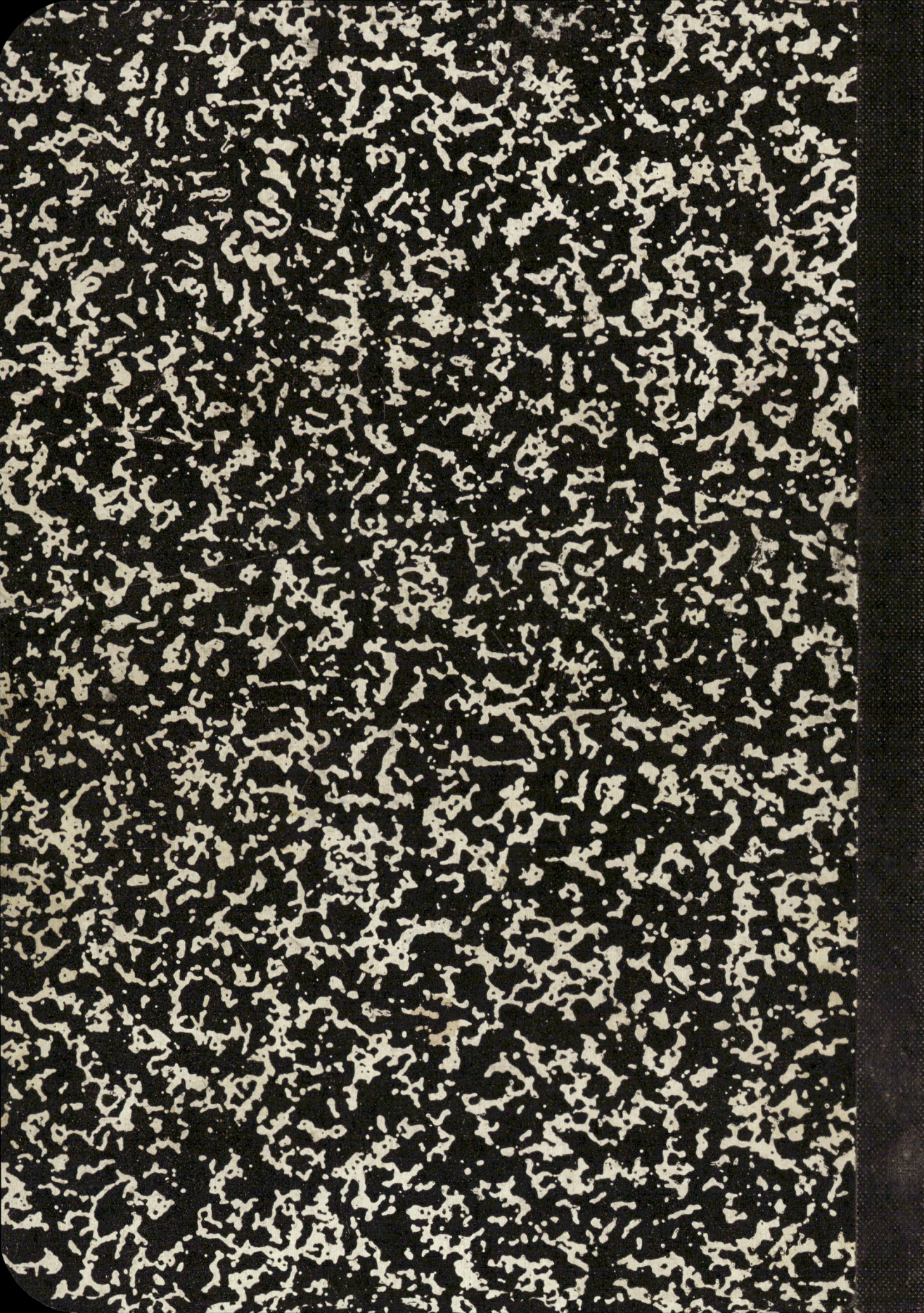

SHE MUST HAVE BEEN A DALLAS GIRL
YANKEES DON'T DRESS LIKE THAT
RIPPED UP JEANS, DENIM SHIRT
BIG OL' COWBOY HAT—

HIS WAFFLE THICK SHOES SMELLED LIKE A COP
OUT ALL HE'D WAS A WALKIE-TALKIE—

THESE GIRLS THEY GET ON THE PHONE
AND JUST DON'T STOP TALKING
THEY JUST YAK IT UP

THEY HAD MULE SPAGHETTI IN PHILS
I THINK I WOULD OF LIKED NEW FRIED

) THE WAIT. THE SERVICE. THE POLITENESS.
THE WAIT. THE DEDICATED COMMITMENT.
THE SOLDIER. THE IDIOT. WE'VE ALL
COME TO WAIT.
IN OUR HOUSES ON THE STREETS
THAT WE DECORATE. AMUSE
DISTRACT OURSELVES WITH.
POSSES. WE LIKE TO POSSES.
TO FORGET THAT WE O ARE
POSSESIONS. SOLDIERS.

THE EATING THE WAY WE
FANCY UP THE FOOD ON THE
PLATE. A DISTRACTION.

HBA

LADIES + GENTLEMEN THIS IS YOUR ~~SUPERFICIAL~~
ANNOUNCER INVITING YOU TO ANOTHER
EPISODE OF
   "CELEBRITY HEROIN ADDICT"!
THE SHOW THAT SAYS "OH, NO! NOT HIM"
"I HAD NO IDEA."

A. WAS A JUNKIE
B. IS STILL A JUNKIE
C. TRYING TO QUIT.

COMPOSITION

CLASS PROGRAM

NAME_____ ADDRESS_____

SCHOOL_____ CLASS_____

	TIME	FROM TO...	PERIOD 1	PERIOD 2	PERIOD 3	PERIOD 4	PERIOD 5	PERIOD 6	PERIOD 7	PERIOD 8
MONDAY	SUBJECT									
	ROOM									
	INSTRUCTOR									
TUESDAY	SUBJECT									
	ROOM									
	INSTRUCTOR									
WEDNESDAY	SUBJECT									
	ROOM									
	INSTRUCTOR									
THURSDAY	SUBJECT									
	ROOM									
	INSTRUCTOR									
FRIDAY	SUBJECT									
	ROOM									
	INSTRUCTOR									
SATURDAY	SUBJECT									
	ROOM									
	INSTRUCTOR									

mead
100 Sheets
9¾ in x 7½ in
24.7 cm x 19.0 cm
Wide Ruled

09910   The Mead Corporation, Dayton, Ohio 45463

THIS IS NOT IN PRAISE OF POISON
ING MYSELF ▪ WAITING FOR IDEAS
TO HAPPEN · MYSELF · THIS ▮▮▮ NOT
IN PRAISE OF POISON   IS THIS IS NOT

                              NON
THE NOUN POISONOUS   POISONED
SO SELF RIGHTOUS   POISONED
NO ONE IS CLEAN
FROM RED MEAT TO WHITE
                         POISON
      IS
THIS NOT IN PRAISE OF ~~POISON~~
THE BIGGEST BUISNESS
UGLY, FAT LIKE A PIG

THE CUSTOMER IN NEW YORK,
CHICAGO DETROIT

PSALM

TRUE STORY

SHOT A FOOL'S ~~HEAD OFF~~

"SHOT A FOOL'S HEAD OFF"!

~~JAILHNG~~

"ANDY'S TRAP
NO DICE
STRICTLY CASH
PIAGET WATCHES"
T

PEDXING

"WHAT ABOUT YELLOW?"

T.C.

A PRAYER

NICOTINE WALKS ON EGGSHELLS
MEDICATED

THE EARTH WAS FOR LE (M)
                    FORMLESS VOID
DARKNESS (K)
DARKNESS FACE OF THE DEEP
SPIRIT MOVED ACROSS THE
WATER AND THERE WAS LIGHT

"IT WAS GOOD" ©

BREATHING INTO HIS LUNGS
2000 YEARS OF ASBESTOS.

WAX SEAL
LINE
STAMP

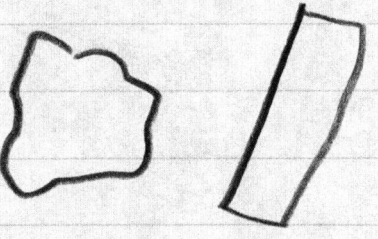

VERY OFFICAL

"FOR THE SICKLES FOR THE MATTOCKS FOR THE FORKS FOR THE AXES" ©

SHINING SHOE IN SAINT LOUIS,

SHINING SHOES IN SAINT

LOVE IS A LIE

LOVER = LIAR

CHEMICAL WATE

DO NOT DRINK
STRICTLY FOR
SUGARCANE

UNABLE TO STING HER
~~OR~~   OR FLY AWAY

"VERY OBVIOUS"
ASKEW
ODD/OFF BASE ©

NEON SHOE REPAIR

LOTTERY
CANDY
MAGAZINES
CIGARS©

"ARAB SINGING"

EFFECTIVE 12:61 AM ©

AN EVIL CAT IN A TOP HAT
COMING OUT OF A SEWER
~~WITH A FIRECR~~
WITH AN M-80

A CAT POURING TACKS
ON HIS TOUNGE ©

CROCODILE AS PIRATE

NEXT OF KIN
LINAMENT
INDIAN CLUBS

A MICKEY FINN WITH
FUZZ ON IT IN A
TURKISH BATH©

ROACH EGGS
ROACH EGGS
ROACH EGGS
ROACH EGGS
ROACH EGGS
ROACH EGGS
ROACH EGGS

PEEL

NOT IN PRAISE

T

NOT IN PRAISE OF POISON

JUNK AND CIGARETTES

~~MADONNA~~
BRUCE WALLACE,
WALTER CRONKITE
JARMUSCH
GODARD
PEE WEE
NICHOLSON
J. HUSTON
ALI
~~AMSTRO~~
JOHN GLENN
MILES DAVIS
KELLE
PRINCE
DAVID LYNCH
WILLIAM BURROWS
ELISABETH TAYLOR
ROBERT DE NIRO
BERNARD GOETZ .
~~R~~ RINGO STAR
~~B~~ ELTON JOAN
STEVE WONDER

AMATEUR BOUT ©

~~N.Y.C.~~

NEW YORK.

ACKNOWLEDGMENTS

The chain of events that brought this book into existence had its starting point in the 1980s. My gratitude extends back in time as well, to those individuals who first encouraged me to collect Jean-Michel's notebooks. Rene Ricard was the catalyst for their acquisition, and I am forever grateful for his insightful, passionate insistence. My thanks to Michael Holman and Nick Taylor, who enabled me to acquire Jean-Michel's notebooks. I am indebted to the late Gerard Basquiat, Jean-Michel's father, for his support and encouragement through the years, and to Nora Fitzpatrick for her many kindnesses. My thanks, too, to Richard Marshall and John Cheim, who were among my colleagues on the Basquiat Authentication Committee.

Many individuals active in the 1980s New York art world enriched my understanding of the art that was taking shape at that time. Among them are Tony Shafrazi and his colleague Hiroko Onoda, Fred Brathwaite, Lenny McGurr, Kenny Scharf, Rich Colicchio, Stephen Lack, Mary-Ann Monforton, and Patti Astor. Others, now gone, were key figures of that time. I fondly salute Keith Haring, Tseng Kwong Chi, Arch Connelly, Kiely Jenkins, Rammellzee, Christine Zonack, and Henry Geldzahler, with whom I spent countless hours talking about Jean-Michel Basquiat.

As always, conversations with Dieter Buchhart have been crucial in my thinking about Jean-Michel and the notebooks, as were my exchanges with Franklin Sirmans and with Jeffrey Deitch, another longtime colleague on the Basquiat Authentication Committee. Carlo McCormick has been a constant source of inspiration, and Henry Louis Gates offered many fresh insights as well. I am deeply grateful to Arnold Lehman and his curators at the Brooklyn Museum, who have nurtured my efforts to bring the work of Jean-Michel and other artists to new generations of viewers. At Princeton University Press, director Peter J. Dougherty has again earned my appreciation and admiration, and the same is true for editor Michelle Komie. My thanks as well to the book's designer, Hannah Alderfer. Special thanks to David Stark for his help and support. In seeing the manuscript through to completion, I am especially grateful to Taliesin Thomas for her research and organization; to Susan Delson for her indispensable editorial guidance; and to Steven Rodriguez for his always-timely assistance. Finally, my profound love and gratitude to the two most important women in my life: my wife Abbey, for the support that means everything to me; and my mother, for always being there for me.

JEAN-MICHEL BASQUIAT (1960–1988) is one of the most important artists of the twentieth century. An American artist born and raised in Brooklyn, NY, his Haitian and Puerto Rican heritage is evident in many of his paintings that reflect his bi-cultural understanding and his passion for the confluence of influences and imagery. As a teenager, Basquiat began creating art full time as one half of the graffiti duo SAMO©, spray painting cryptic phrases on walls and found objects around New York City. Around 1980, Basquiat's work began attracting attention in the art world where he quickly rose to fame until his untimely death in 1988.

Basquiat has been the subject of several major retrospectives including exhibitions at the Whitney Museum of American Art, the Serpentine Gallery, the Brooklyn Museum, the Barbican Gallery, the National Gallery of Victoria, the Mori Arts Center Gallery, the Museum of Fine Arts, Boston, the Fondation Louis Vuitton, and the Fondation Beyeler, among other notable international venues. His work resides in the permanent collections of major museums and private collections around the world.

LARRY WARSH has been active in the art world for more than thirty years as a publisher and artist-collaborator. Warsh was a lead organizer for the exhibition *Basquiat: The Unknown Notebooks*, which debuted at the Brooklyn Museum, New York, in 2015, and later traveled to several American museums. The original notebooks were also included in the exhibitions at the Mori Arts Center Gallery, Tokyo, the National Gallery of Victoria, Melbourne, and the Museum of Fine Arts, Boston. Warsh was instrumental in publishing multiple translations of the notebooks in conjunction with these exhibitions, including editions in Japanese, French and Mandarin.

The founder of Museums Magazine, Warsh has been involved in many publishing projects, including *Keith Haring: 31 Subway Drawings*, and is the editor of several other titles published by Princeton University Press, including *Basquiat-isms* (2019), *Haring-isms* (2020), *Futura-isms* (2021), *Abloh-isms* (2021), and *Arsham-isms* (2021), among others. Warsh has served on the board of the Getty Museum Photographs Council and was a founding member of the Basquiat Authentication Committee until its dissolution in 2012.

NO MORE RULERS (NMR) is a platform representing empowerment, respect, and progression in the art world. NMR partners with leading international institutions, legacy artists, and estates to validate creators through channels of connection, exhibition, and distribution. By connecting audiences with narratives from both top creators and new voices, NMR hopes to empower the creative community and help rethink the status quo.

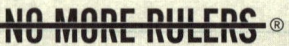